TRUE CRIME COLLECTION

GRIPPING ENCOUNTERS WITH SERIAL KILLERS
BOOK 1

JAMIE MALTON

MP
Malton
Publishing
LLC

MaltonPublishing.com

WORD OF WARNING

The details written in these stories come directly from eyewitness accounts, interviews, court transcripts, crime scenes, and autopsy reports. Due to the graphic nature of the crimes featured in *Killer Case Files* which include murder, domestic violence, sexual assault, hate crimes, sex work, incest, mental illness, child abuse, animal abuse, abduction, suicide, mutilation, and necrophilia, reader discretion is advised.

CANYON LAKE MURDERS

THE MAIN STREET TRADING POST, LAKE ELSINORE, CALIFORNIA 1994

Fifty-seven-year-old Dorinda Hawkins watched the young blonde woman walk into her store. She briefly locked eyes with her to see if she needed help. The blonde averted her gaze and walked to a shelf containing silver picture frames. Dorinda assumed the woman was browsing the antique store and left her alone.

After several minutes, the woman spoke and told Dorinda she was looking for picture frames for several photos of her mother. Then she asked Dorinda if she was alone in the store. At the time, Dorinda didn't think the question odd and invited the woman to the back of the store to show her a more extensive selection of frames. None of the frames interested the woman, so Dorinda placed them back on a shelf. It was then that she felt something soft around her neck, followed by a hard pull, and realized that the woman was trying to choke her.

Dorinda tried to turn around and look at the woman, but she was too strong and stayed behind her, pulling the ligature tighter. The woman had a long yellow rope, and Dorinda could see knots tied in its length. As they struggled, Dorinda asked her, "Why? Why do you want to kill me? I have eight children!"

The woman said nothing and pushed Dorinda down on the floor, stepping on her head to pull the ligature harder and cut off the older woman's air supply. Dorinda managed to grab a nearby broom and poke the woman with the handle to no avail.

The woman said softly, "Relax. Just relax."

In her final conscious moments, Dorinda realized she was dying at the hands of someone who had killed before.

Forty minutes later, Dorinda regained consciousness and called the police. When they arrived, she discovered money from her wallet was missing, and the store's cash register was empty. While the police initially wrote the crime off as a simple assault and robbery, Dorinda Hawkins wasn't surprised to learn later that she was the one surviving victim of serial killer Dana Sue Gray.

~

Dana Sue Gray was born as Dana Sue Armbrust on December 6th, 1957, to Beverly and Russell Armbrust in Southern California. Her father was a hairdresser with three previous marriages, and her mother was a former beauty queen and MGM Starlet. Beverly Armbrust was described as an aggressive and vain woman, and according to her friends, she had trouble controlling her temper.

Dana's parents ended their marriage when Dana was two years old. Russell couldn't handle Beverly's excessive spending or her temper. One day, after breaking up a physical altercation between Beverly and an elderly neighbor, he decided he'd had enough.

Dana had little contact with her father over the next several years, and Beverly's skills fell short as a parent. She was emotionally unavailable, opting to buy gifts for her daughter rather than offer love.

Dana struggled in school and often fought with other children. Her grades were poor, and she was frequently suspended for forging notes to skip school.
To gain more attention at home, Dana started stealing money for candy whenever Beverly disciplined her. She would also get physically violent with her mother.

TEENAGE TURNING POINT

Dana Sue's life changed at the age of 14 when her mother was diagnosed with breast cancer. The experience of watching nurses care for her ailing mother inspired Dana to pursue a career in nursing. After Beverly died in 1975, Dana, still a teenager, moved in with her father but was soon thrown out of the house after her stepmother, Geri Davis Armbrust, discovered drugs in her room.

Dana moved in with Rob, an older man who was a sky-diving instructor until she graduated from high school. Rob paid for her nursing school and taught her to skydive, adding a touch of adventure to her life. During this period, she became pregnant twice, and on both occasions, Rob persuaded her to end the pregnancies. In 1981, Dana left Rob after graduating from nursing school.

LIFE WITH TOM GRAY

Her life took a promising turn in October 1987 when Dana married Tom Gray, a fellow sports enthusiast who had admired her since high school. Their wedding was held at an upscale winery in the Temecula area. Dana worked as a labor and delivery nurse at Inland Valley Regional Medical Center, and she and Tom lived in the gated community of Canyon Lake. Dana got pregnant several times during her marriage, but each pregnancy ended in miscarriage.

THE SPIRAL DOWN

While Dana was employed and made a good wage, she and her husband started several businesses, all of which failed. She enjoyed her luxurious lifestyle in the gated community of Canyon Lake and continued to spend heavily even though it put a strain on her marriage. Dana and Tom were forced to file for bankruptcy in September 1993 to stave off foreclosure on their Canyon Lake home.

Dana became depressed and self-medicated with alcohol and a variety of drugs obtained from her workplace. Her relationship with her husband was failing, and she started an affair with their mutual friend, Jim Wilkins. She eventually moved in with Wilkins and his young son, Jason, when the bank foreclosed on her Canyon Lake home. Wilkins was an out-of-work machinist and lived in a trailer with his son.

In November 1993, she was fired from the hospital for misappropriating Demerol and other opiate painkillers and was unable to get another job, but her desire to spend money hadn't waned. With no job, Dana started making and selling screen-printed t-shirts she made in Wilkins' home.

THE MURDERS

On February 14th, 1994, Dana arranged to meet her estranged husband, saying she only wanted to talk with him. Tom Gray originally agreed to meet her but then changed his mind, a decision which may have saved his life. Dana had taken out a six-figure life insurance policy on him, and later that day, Dana committed her first of three murders.

MURDER ONE

Geri Davis Armbrust, the stepmother who'd thrown Dana out of the house as a teenager, had a former mother-in-law, 86-year-old Norma Davis. Dana knew the older woman well and had even stayed at her Canyon Lake house as a teenager.

Norma, recovering from triple bypass surgery, was found dead in her home by a friend. She had a utility knife protruding from her neck and a fillet knife sticking out of her chest two and was still in her robe and slippers, sitting in her recliner. Police found no sign of forced entry, suggesting she knew her attacker. They also found a Nike shoe print near the body that didn't belong to Norma.

The suspicion fell on Geri Armbrust in the case of Norma Davis's murder. Detectives learned that Geri had continued to care for her former mother-in-law after she divorced her son. They found it unusual that Geri would care for someone who was not a blood relative, especially after she married Russell Armbrust, Dana Sue Gray's father. Geri also wore Nikes, the same brand of shoe that left a print at the crime scene. However, after weeks of interactions, lead investigator Detective Joseph Greco realized that Geri Armbrust was not the killer. Eventually, his conversations with Geri would steer him toward the actual perpetrator, Dana Sue Gray.

MURDER TWO

The second victim was June Roberts, a 66-year-old woman who lived in the same gated community as Norma. Even though Dana had lost her Canyon Lake home to foreclosure, she could still open the neighborhood access gate with the sticker on her Cadillac. Dana had visited Roberts under the pretense of borrowing a book about controlling a drinking problem. She had five-year-old Jason with her and left him inside the car in the driveway, telling him she'd be a few minutes. Once June let Dana in the house and shut the door behind her, Dana turned violent, strangling Roberts to death with a phone cord and subsequently stealing her credit cards.

She took Jason shopping with her and bought him a toy. Then she went to a spa where Dana had an eyebrow wax and dyed her hair red. As Jason got a haircut, Dana told the clerk she was on a shopping spree. She used June's credit card when it was time to pay the spa bill. The pair moved on to Temecula and had a lavish lunch in a cafe. Dana over-ordered, and the food was wrapped to go. Dana's use of June's credit cards was so prolific that the credit card company alerted Roberts' family, leading detectives to the stores where Dana had made her purchases. As they interviewed the cashiers, they began to piece together a physical description of their murderer and learned crucial details, such as her recent hair dye job from blonde to red and the presence of a little boy named Jason.

With two murders in the community, Canyon Lake residents felt threatened and sought safety by vacating their homes temporarily and choosing to stay with other family members until the mystery of the murders was resolved. A group of elderly widows forged a pact of communal living, sleeping in large groups at designated houses. The police had no concrete answers for the scared Canyon Lake residents.

Russell and Geri Armbrust, Dana's father and step-mother, also lived in Canyon Lake. They were upset by the loss of their acquaintance, June Roberts, and Geri's former mother-in-law, Norma Davis. They were also frightened, and Russell kept a loaded gun with him at all times. Dana had visited them the day before almost unrecognizable, with her hair dyed red. Dana needed more money and pleaded with her father for financial help — a request he denied. They didn't realize that Dana had already murdered two women and was on her way to Lake Elsinore to an antique store where she would attempt to murder Dorinda Hawkins to feed her overwhelming need to shop.

After the police were able to interview survivor Dorinda Hawkins thoroughly, they realized her attack was likely perpetrated by the same person who'd murdered Norma Davis and June Roberts. Geri Armbrust was asked to look at a police sketch drawn from Hawkins's account since Geri knew both murdered women. The woman in the drawing seemed familiar, and when she heard from police that June Roberts' murderer had taken her credit cards, gone on a shopping spree, changed her hair color, and had a young boy with her, she told Detective Greco the woman they wanted was her own stepdaughter, Dana Sue Gray.

FINAL MURDER

This crucial information led Detective Greco to get a search warrant for Dana's home in Lake Elsinore, where she was living with Jim Wilkins, and he had a team of officers watching her house. Unbeknownst to the team, on the very day that they began their surveillance, March 16th, 1994, Gray was murdering her final victim, Dora Beebe. Dana approached Beebe under the guise of needing directions, and 87-year-old Beebe, in a gesture of kindness, invited Dana inside her Lake Elsinore home to look at a map. Once inside, Dana attacked and killed Beebe by strangling her with a phone cord and then hitting her in the head with an iron. Just like with

Roberts, Dana used Beebe's credit cards for a shopping spree shortly after the murder.

Dana was now being followed, and police observed her using Beebe's card at a bank and embarking on another shopping spree. She cashed a check on Beebe's bank account for $2000 and signed it *Dana Beebe*. She shopped at a gourmet grocery store and bought several bottles of supplements at a health food store. They had enough evidence to link Dana to Beebe's murder. Later that day, Detective Greco arrested her while she was cooking dinner for her family.

During questioning, Gray initially denied taking the credit cards. When faced with evidence of using them, she claimed she had found both Roberts' and Beebe's cards. She stuck to this story for hours, insisting that she had kept the cards due to an overwhelming need to shop and showing no apparent sympathy for her victims.

Despite her reluctance to confess, the weight of the evidence was undeniable. Detective Greco eventually booked Gray for murdering June Roberts and Dora Beebee, but they felt like they didn't have enough evidence to charge her for the death of Norma Davis. At a hearing on July 23rd, Deputy DA Richard Bentley requested the death penalty.

Gray initially pleaded insanity on all counts. However, after a witness claimed to have seen Gray at Roberts' house on the day of her death, Gray changed her plea.

She pleaded guilty to robbing and murdering two women and attempting to murder another. By pleading guilty, Gray avoided the death penalty.

Gray's confessions of her crimes always started with how the women angered her, which triggered her to kill. According to Dana, June Roberts had criticized her marriage and told Dana she should have tried harder in her relationship with Tom Gray. She also handed her the wrong book, which Dana said angered her even more. Dana said Dora Beebe complained about helping her, saying she didn't have time to show her where to go on the map. And finally, Dorinda Hawkins, the surviving victim, looked down on her by crossing her arms when she walked into the antique store.

FOUR YEARS LATER

During the trial, expert testimony from two forensic psychiatrists testified that Dana's mental state met the criteria for legal insanity. One doctor diagnosed Dana's condition as a severe psychotic depression complicated by chronic alcoholism. Another doctor added "unspeci-fied dissociative disorder." This disorder, according to the psychiatrist, may have led Dana to confuse her victims with the figure of her abusive mother from childhood.

The prosecution's psychiatrist diagnosed Dana with borderline personality disorder and pointed out that she had never been hospitalized for mental illness. The prosecution pointed to the fact that Dana wore plastic gloves when she committed the murders, which implied premeditation.

Dana Sue Gray made a statement in court. "My life and my career have been focused on healing. It has strayed so far from that goal it was so out of character. I'm sorry, and I know that these words will never be enough. I will live with this the rest of my life."

On October 16, 1998, Dana Sue Gray was sentenced to life in prison without parole. For money, she occasionally sells items to people who collect murderabilia, which are items belonging to known murderers. A recent item that sold for $250 was a pair of white panties labeled with the name Dana Sue Gray and her prisoner number, W76776, written in black marker across the crotch. Her shopping is now confined to the prisoner store at the California Women's Prison in Chowchilla.

JUSTICE DELAYED

TEXAS

On a balmy May evening in 1997, 19-year-old Sandra
Sapaugh pulled her car up to a gas station's payphone.
The light was fading fast as she rummaged through her
purse for some change to call a friend.

Across the street, a man watched Sandra from behind
the wheel of a white truck; when she briefly went inside
the convenience store to make a purchase, the man
punctured her car tire with a knife.

Sandra left the store, unaware she was being watched
and returned to her car. The engine hummed to life, and
she drove off, not noticing the air slowly leaking out of
her tire or the white truck that had pulled out onto the
highway behind her.

Minutes down the road, her steering wheel jerked to one side, and she heard a thump. By the time she pulled off the highway, she realized the thumping sound was a flat tire. She had no spare, so her only option was to walk back to the station and get some help.

Just as she got out of the car, the white truck's headlights appeared behind her, and a man got out of the truck. "Need a hand?" he asked with a smile. Relief washed over Sandra as she accepted his offer of a ride back to the gas station.

She climbed into the passenger seat of his truck, her pulse rate finally calming from the scare of the flat tire. Once the door was shut and locked, the man's demeanor changed. He pulled a knife and told Sandra to undress. He held her down forcefully. With a piece of rope, he tied her hands tightly before restarting the truck and driving off with his prisoner.

As the truck drove on, Sandra writhed against her restraints, crying. She had a child at home, and she was pregnant. She knew if she didn't try to escape, she may never see her child again. She also decided if she was going to die, she would do it on her terms. With a strength she didn't know she possessed, Sandra broke free from her bindings and shook the ropes from her wrists. Seizing her moment of freedom, she did the unthinkable — she flung open the truck door and leaped from the moving vehicle into the night.

She hit the pavement hard, unable to stop rolling as the truck's taillights faded into the distance. She was sure the man would return for her so she got up and started running. She made it to safety when a genuine Good Samaritan picked her up and took her to the hospital. The police were called, and she told them what she could. She had blacked out, but she and the baby were fine.

A few months later, in a police line-up, Sandra was able to identify the man who had abducted her. She pointed to William Lewis Reece without hesitation. At this point, neither Sandra nor the police realized that her abductor was partially responsible for the infamous *Texas Killing Fields* body count.

The Texas Killing Fields are a desolate and remote area along Interstate 45 between Houston and Galveston, Texas. The area spanning roughly 50 acres is notorious for the high number of bodies found there since the 1970s. It has been nicknamed the *serial killer's playground*. The desolate nature of the terrain, combined with its proximity to the highway, has made it easy for killers to dispose of their victims and difficult for law enforcement to patrol.

$\sim$

William Lewis Reece was born on July 1st, 1959, in Oklahoma, into a family of sixteen. And because the family was so big, he and his thirteen siblings were often forced to live in terrible conditions as his parents struggled to make ends meet. William had behavioral issues as a child and was sent to a boy's home for a brief period. As a teenager, he left school after the ninth grade to get a job as a farm laborer.

While doing farm work, he met Judy Flaming, also from Oklahoma. Their dates quickly became a passionate affair, leading to Judy's pregnancy. Judy's parents did not want her to marry William, even with a child on the way, but she did anyway. In 1979, Judy and William exchanged vows in a Gracemont church.

Not long after the nuptials, William enlisted in the Oklahoma National Guard. He left after finding out the military lifestyle didn't suit him. Following the birth of their child, William changed and wanted nothing to do with his family. He and Judy divorced one year after they were married. Now alone, William realized he'd made a mistake and convinced Judy to marry him again. They had another child and appeared to be happy for a while.

As time went on, William started drinking, sometimes heavily, and he would physically abuse Judy. In 1982, Judy went to the police and told them her husband had threatened to kill her with a knife and a shotgun. She was scared he would harm the children. She divorced him again not long after, but the abuse didn't stop. William, no longer living with the family, would show up at Judy's home with a gun, threaten Judy, and beat her in front of the children.

One year, he forced them to attend a Thanksgiving dinner at a relative's home, and William again pulled a gun on Judy and threatened to kill her. William moved from Oklahoma to Texas, and the family abuse stopped for Judy Flaming and her children, but it started anew for more women, and this time, William made good on his threats to kill.

ACCELERATION OF VIOLENCE

William didn't want to quell his growing desire for violence. In April of 1986, he kidnapped the 19-year-old daughter of a local sheriff's deputy while she was driving to the gym. William worked as a truck driver at the time, and he saw that her car had broken down, so he was able to lure her into his truck with the promise of a ride.

Just like with Sandra Sapaugh, once the girl was in his car, William tied her up, and he immediately sexually assaulted her. He kept her tied, took her to a nearby motel, and assaulted her again. She begged him to let her use the bathroom, and while she was alone in there, she was able to escape through the window and go to the police.

William was arrested, though he would be released on bail. While on bail, he sexually assaulted another woman and was arrested again. William was tried for both sexual assault and ultimately sentenced to 25 years behind bars.

His attorneys got his sentence reduced on an appeal after a judge determined procedural errors were made during the original case. He was released on parole in October of 1996 after serving nine years in prison.

THE FIRST MURDER

In early 1997, after regaining his driver's license, William moved to Houston, Texas, where he committed his first murder, marking the beginning of a horrifying series of crimes. That murder took place on April 3rd when he killed Laura Smither, 12, after accidentally hitting her with his car while driving around in Friendswood. In an attempt to cover up the incident, he took the injured girl to a nearby lake and strangled her before dumping her body in the water.

Two months after his unsuccessful attempt to kidnap Sandra Sapaugh on I-45, he committed another murder. He was returning to Houston from a visit to his mother in Oklahoma when he stopped at a Denton gas station to purchase whiskey. There, he encountered Kelli Cox, a young mother and University of North Texas student, and following an argument and a physical fight, he strangled her. He buried her body in Brazoria County's woods, though he later denied sexually assaulting her. Her body wasn't found until 2007.

Only eleven days later, on July 26th, 1997, he committed another murder. At the Sunshine Car Wash in Bethany,

Oklahoma, he encountered Tiffany Johnston. Realizing no one else was around the car wash, he abducted her, sexually assaulted her at gunpoint, and then killed her using a horseshoe. Her body was disposed of in nearby woods.

On August 17th, 1997, he targeted Jessica Cain, 17, outside a Bennigan's restaurant in Clear Lake City, a Houston suburb. After she initially refused to get into his truck and drove away, he pursued and forced her off the road, then violently murdered her. He buried Cain's body in the Killing fields.

The police eventually arrested William for the kidnapping of Sandra Sapaugh. In the subsequent trial, he received a 60-year prison sentence.

In 2015, authorities, having grown suspicious of his involvement in other Houston-area disappearances, conducted DNA tests that linked him to Tiffany Johnston's murder. In 2015, he was charged with her murder. He cooperated with investigators to avoid the death penalty in Texas, confessing to three additional murders from the summer of 1997. He assisted with locating the bodies, all found in the Texas Killing Fields.

His trial in Oklahoma was delayed due to asbestos contamination at the courthouse and was further postponed by the COVID-19 pandemic. The trial eventually started in May 2021 with Sandra Sapaugh and the relatives of Tiffany Johnston present in the courtroom.

The prosecution laid out a compelling narrative advocating for the death penalty in the sentencing phase of William's trial. They painted a picture of a man whose history was marred by violent felonies, and they claimed this pattern would continue.

They discussed the cruel nature of Tiffany Johnston's murder and said William had murdered her to silence her, to prevent her from ever testifying against him. They claimed he would go to any lengths, including murder, to escape justice and should be sentenced to death. On May 28th, 2021, William Reece was given the death penalty for the murder of Tiffany Johnston.

He was moved back to Texas, where he was tried and received three life sentences for the murders of Jessica Cain, Laurie Smither, and Kelli Cox.

William Reece, now in his 60s, continues to serve his 60-year sentence for the kidnapping of Sandra Sapaugh.

Given the stipulations of the extradition agreement he signed in Texas, which require him to serve any sentence imposed in Oklahoma only after completing his term in Texas, it seems unlikely that he will ever be extradited back to Oklahoma for execution for the murder of Tiffany Johnston.

PLAYGROUND PREDATOR

Westley Allan Dodd kept a notebook in his apartment to write down his thoughts and desires. He also chronicled his attempts to actively stalk, abduct, sexually abuse, and murder children.

The pages contained plans and schematic drawings of exactly how he wanted to torture and kill young children. In it, he used words like "torture rack" and "experimental surgery."

It was not all a fantasy for Dodd. Unfortunately, it was very real as the notebook also contained writings about the final moments and hours of several young children. His writings were unflinching, and his indifference towards his child victims was startling.

From Dodd's Diary; The Abduction of Lee Iseli in Portland, Or.

"Sunday, October 29, 1989

10:30 a.m. Left home.

10:45 a.m. Bought film for Polaroid camera.

11:30 a.m. At the school I found yesterday evening saw two 8- 9-year-olds and a 4 -5-year-old a little ways away. Watched a few minutes and decided not to risk it.

11:48 a.m. Arrived at park.

12:15 p.m. No signs of any children.

12:43 p.m. Back at school. Three 8- 9-year-olds and one 4- or maybe 5-year-old. Circled school (drove around block) and thought an adult showed up with another 3- 4-year-old. Park on opposite side of school from kids--adult turned out to be only about 12-years-old.

I stood against a pole. The big kid and his 3-4-year-old brother left. Two 8- 9-year-olds were playing ball and heading toward the far end of the school. The other 8-9-year-old was sitting on a post watching them, the backs of the older three toward me and the 4- 5-year-old playing on a mound 20 feet to my left. I went up to the little boy and asked him if he wanted to "have some fun and make some money." He seemed unsure but not scared. I said, "Come on — this will be fun," and reached out my hand. He took it and walked to the end of the building with me — we got out of sight of the other kids unseen.

I told him as we kept walking, hand-in-hand, "We're going to get in my car." He said, "I don't want any money." I picked him up and said, "We're still going — let's go ask your dad if you can go with me." We got to my car. I put him in the driver's side. As we drove away, he said, "I live the other way." I said, "We're going to my house and play some games — just do what I tell you, and I promise I won't hurt you."

12:50 p.m. A couple blocks from the school I asked and he said his name was Lee, and he was 4 years old. He started to cry a couple times, but I reached out and held his hand, assuring him he'd be okay and that we'd have some fun."

According to Dodd's diary, he kept Lee alive until the next morning. He sexually assaulted the boy several times at his apartment and then took him to a store where he bought him a toy. Lee cried in front of a clerk in the store, but Dodd explained he was the boy's uncle, and they left. Afterward, they went to McDonald's for dinner.

Back at the apartment, Dodd watched Lee play with the new toy and wrote notes in his notebook. Throughout the night, he continued to sexually assault the child and finally strangled him to unconsciousness, only to revive him and kill him by hanging him with a rope in his closet. Dodd documented his assaults and murder with his Polaroid camera before and after the child's murder and left the child hanging in the closet while he was at work before disposing of the body.

On November 1st, a pheasant hunter came across the naked body of a young boy at the edge of Vancouver Lake in Vancouver, Washington. The remains were later identified as belonging to Lee Iseli.

~

Westley Allan Dodd was born in Toppenish, Washington on July 3rd, 1961. He was the eldest of three children born to Jim and Carol Dodd. His childhood, as he would later claim, was devoid of any physical abuse or neglect, yet it was marked by an emotional void. It was a house with no familial affection, and Dodd noted that the words "I love you" were never expressed to him, nor did he recall uttering them.

Dodd claimed his father was a physically abusive figure, and he witnessed many violent altercations between his parents. On Dodd's 15th birthday, his father attempted suicide following a dispute with his wife.

He wrote in a diary that his parents favored his other siblings, and he felt neglected. Dodd's isolation extended beyond his home and into his school, where he was ostracized and friendless. By the age of nine, he had already discovered a sexual attraction toward other boys, a desire that would later define his adult life.

Despite the turbulence at home, Dodd graduated from Richland High School in 1979, marking the end of his tumultuous childhood and the beginning of a life that would soon take a dark turn.

There is only Dodd's account of what happened in his early years, but it's notable that his younger brother, Gregory, was also arrested in 2016 for the attempted sexual abuse of a 13-year-old girl. The "girl" was an undercover police officer in Gulfport, Mississippi, and Gregory Dodd was given a four-year prison sentence and is a registered sex offender. This alarming detail raises questions about the unknown dynamics within the Dodd family.

CRIMINAL ACTIVITIES BEGIN

Dodd's criminal history began to manifest at a young age. At 13, he started exposing himself to children in his neighborhood. According to Dodd, his father was aware of this behavior and chose to ignore it because Dodd was a "well-behaved child" who never grappled with drugs, drinking, or smoking.

By the time he reached high school, Dodd's actions had progressed to child sex abuse with his younger cousins and neighborhood children, whom he offered to babysit.

Despite an arrest for indecent exposure at the age of 15, his only consequence was a recommendation for juvenile counseling.

In August 1981, when Dodd was 20, he attempted to abduct two girls. They reported him to the police, but no action was taken. The following month, he enlisted in the US Navy, where he found a new hunting ground at the submarine base in Bangor, Washington. He began abusing children who lived on the base, continuing his pattern of offending without consequences.

Dodd's behavior escalated when he propositioned a group of boys with $50 to play a game of strip poker in a motel room. Arrested once more, he confessed to his plan to molest the boys but was released with no charges filed. His criminal activity continued unabated, leading to another arrest for exposing himself to a boy. His only consequence was a dishonorable discharge from the Navy and a brief incarceration.

He carefully planned his life around gaining easy access to children. He moved into an apartment block with families, took jobs at fast-food restaurants, and worked as a charity truck driver. The pre-school-aged children of a neighbor became his repeated victims, but their mother declined to press charges, fearing the trauma that the experience might impose on her children.

In 1987, Dodd's attempts at luring a young boy into a vacant building were thwarted when the boy refused and reported him to the police. Despite prosecutors recommending a five-year prison sentence, Dodd once again received minimal punishment because he hadn't physically touched the boy or exposed himself. He was placed on probation and ordered to seek psychiatric treatment. After his probation, he stopped attending treatment and moved to Vancouver, Washington.

During the early autumn of 1989, Dodd identified David Douglas Park in Vancouver as a prime location to find potential victims. Over the next few years, he was arrested multiple times for child molestation, serving short jail sentences and receiving court-mandated therapy. His victims were always children, around 50 in total, all under the age of 12, with some as young as 2, and most of them boys. Dodd claimed that boys were less likely to tell adults about the abuse. One psychiatrist who evaluated him after one of his convictions labeled him a "sexual psychopath."

MURDERS

Dodd's sexual fantasies grew increasingly violent, and he began to harbor thoughts of murder. The year 1989 marked a horrific turning point in Dodd's offenses. His decades-long pattern of child sexual abuse escalated to murder, and his victims were three young boys in Vancouver, Washington.

The first to tragically cross paths with Dodd were

brothers Cole and William Neer, aged 11 and 10, respectively. Dodd detailed the murders in his notebook. He lured the two boys to a secluded area under the pretense of showing them a "neat spot." He tied them up with shoestrings and assaulted Cole first. He tried to assault William but couldn't because the child was crying too hard. Dodd stabbed each of the boys with a knife he carried in his sock, and Cole died on the spot. William managed to briefly run away and scream, "I'm sorry! I'm sorry!" Dodd caught up to him and stabbed him again in the chest and the back, and William succumbed to his wounds. Dodd removed the shoelaces from the boys and calmly departed.

Four-year-old Lee Iseli was Dodd's third and final victim. Lee was at the playground with his older brother, who didn't notice when he walked away with Dodd.

CATCHING THE KILLER

Dodd's murderous spree came to an unexpected halt in 1989 when he tried to abduct another child.

Two weeks after the brutal murder of Lee Iseli, Dodd chose a movie theater in Camas, Washington, for his next victim. The movie playing was the family film, *Honey, I Shrunk the Kids*, but Dodd was far from an ordinary moviegoer. His predatory gaze scanned the dark theater, not for enjoyment of the film, but for his next victim.

His sights fell upon James Kirk, a six-year-old boy, who had left his seat unaccompanied to make his way to the restroom. When the child got up, so did Dodd, and like a shadow, Dodd trailed after him. Once inside the restroom, Dodd hoisted the boy onto his shoulder, intending to make a swift exit. However, Kirk's spirited resistance to the kidnapping, with a cacophony of screams and kicking, alerted bystanders that something was wrong.

In a frantic bid to escape, Dodd dropped the child and dashed outside toward his yellow Ford Pinto. The child's screams had alerted William Graves, the boyfriend of Kirk's mother. Once he saw that Kirk was okay, he raced out the door after the fleeing Dodd.

Dodd was already driving away, but his car failed him blocks from the theater. Graves sprinted after the car, quickly reaching the stalled fugitive. He hauled him out of the Pinto and put him in a chokehold, threatening to break Dodd's neck and telling him he was making a citizen's arrest.

Graves dragged Dodd back to the theater with a strength fueled by adrenaline. Other witnesses joined in, restraining Dodd with a belt until the police arrived.

Once Dodd was questioned, he confessed to the murders of Lee Iseli and Cole and William Neer. He was charged with three counts of aggravated murder in the first degree, with one count of attempted murder in the first degree of James Kirk and one count of kidnapping in the first degree. Dodd initially pleaded not guilty to all charges and sought to suppress his confessions. Once the evidence of his notebooks was introduced in a special hearing, he changed his plea to guilty.

THE APARTMENT

The police searched Dodd's home, and it revealed a cache of incriminating evidence. Dodd's modest and neat apartment contained a collection of Parent/Child books and a copy of the New Testament, which had the inscription, "Satan Lives." Several X-Acto knives lay in a drawer intended for the unspeakable "experimental surgeries" Dodd wrote about in his notebook. Dodd had modified the single bed he slept in with ropes on the headboard and footboard for constraint. The torture rack he'd fashioned out of wood hadn't been used yet and sat against one wall in the bedroom.

Dodd's briefcase found under the bed harbored the most damning evidence. The first sight to confront the officers was the neatly folded "Ghostbusters" underwear belonging to Lee Iseli. Underneath that lay Dodd's notebooks containing his dark fantasies and the details of the three children he murdered.

There were dozens of photos of unclothed children that Dodd had taken himself. It is estimated in his lifetime that, he sexually assaulted more than 175 children.

Westley Allan Dodd asked for the death penalty at his trial, saying, "I must be executed before I have an opportunity to escape or kill someone else. If I do escape, I promise you I will kill and rape again, and I will enjoy every minute of it."

Throughout the trial, Dodd showed a chilling indifference to the evidence presented.

Following a trial that lasted just four days, Dodd was sentenced to death. He requested execution by hanging, a method he believed matched the severity of his actions.

EXECUTION

In the early hours of January 5th, 1993, Westley Allan Dodd was executed at the Washington State Penitentiary in Walla Walla. The execution was carried out before a select group of witnesses, including members of the media, law enforcement, and relatives of Dodd's victims. As the black hood was placed over his head and the noose tightened around his neck, Dodd's final moments were marked by the same chilling indifference he had displayed throughout his trial.

His execution marked the first legal hanging in the United States since 1965.

MOVING TO KANSAS CITY

In 1984, 19-year-old **Paula Godfrey** secured a job shortly after finishing school. John Robinson employed her as a sales representative for his business, Equi II. Robinson offered Godfrey an additional opportunity. He wanted to fly her and several other female recruits to San Antonio, Texas, for a clerical skills training program. Godfrey knew this would help her with her business career aspirations, and she accepted.

The trip to the airport never occurred. She disappeared after John picked up Godfrey from her house in Overland Park, Kansas. A few days after her disappearance, Paula's family was surprised to receive a typed letter from her. The message assured her family she was well, but she no longer wanted contact with them. When she didn't check into the hotel in Texas, her family filed a missing person's report. The family also suspected that the letter wasn't from Godfrey. Because she was an adult, the Overland Park Police Department decided to close the investigation into her case.

It is believed that Paula Godfrey became the first of several victims of John Robinson, infamously dubbed *The Slavemaster,* and one of the first known Internet serial killers.

John Edward Robinson was born to parents Henry and Alberta on December 27, 1943, in Cicero, Illinois. His father was an abusive alcoholic, and his mother a strict disciplinarian, a deadly combination for the psyche of any young boy. He was the middle child of five and did everything he could to stand out, including becoming an Eagle Scout who met Queen Elizabeth II in London.

Once John reached high school, he enrolled at Quigley Preparatory Seminary in Chicago, where he spent time training to be a priest. However, one year later, he dropped out due to disciplinary issues. School records from the time showed him to be a poor student who often ended up in fights with other kids. His behavior hadn't improved by the time he enrolled at Morton Junior College in 1961. He only lasted two years there before dropping out.

MARRIAGE TO NANCY JO LYNCH

In 1964, he moved to Kansas City and married Nancy Jo Lynch, with whom he would have four children: John Jr.,

Kimberley, Christopher, and Christine. Five years after marrying Nancy, he was arrested for embezzling $33,000 from a medical practice where he had worked as a radiographer using forged credentials.

John was sentenced to three years of probation for this but violated that probation only one year later when he moved to Chicago without his probation officer's permission. Once in Chicago, he got a job as an insurance salesman at the R.B. Jones Company, where he embezzled more money. After discovering this, he was ordered to return to Kansas City, where he conducted a securities fraud and mail fraud operation. That operation earned him an extension on his existing probation but no time in prison.

John was a scoutmaster, baseball coach, and Sunday school teacher outside of his criminal activities. He was also named to the board of directors for a local charitable organization. Even there, however, he continued to break the law by forging letters from the executive director, which he used to get himself awarded the organization's Man of the Year.

In 1979, after his probation, John was arrested again for embezzlement and check forgery, which earned him 60 days in prison. After being released, he continued to commit financial crimes, stealing $35,000 from a friend with whom he had formed a bogus hydroponics business.

By 1984, John was still operating in the same manner, having established two fraudulent shell companies. One was Equi II, the company for which Paula Godfrey would soon be hired. After Godfrey disappeared, the police questioned John, as he was the last person known to have seen her. He denied any knowledge of her whereabouts.

John Robinson murdered again one year later. After meeting 19-year-old **Lisa Stasi** and her four-year-old daughter, Tiffany, at a shelter for homeless women in Kansas City, he offered her a spot in an outreach program to help her get a fresh start.

Soon after, Lisa and her daughter were checked into Room 131 at the Rodeway Inn in Overland Park. A few weeks later, while being driven from her sister-in-law's house back to the motel room by John, she and her daughter disappeared.

Lisa's daughter, Tiffany, reappeared shortly after when John contacted his own brother, who had been unable to conceive a child with his wife, and informed him of a young child available for adoption. He told his brother the child's mother had killed herself. For $5,500 in "legal fees," John arranged the adoption using forged signatures and transferred custody of Tiffany to his brother, who was unaware of the actual circumstances behind this.

In January of 1987, two years after Lisa Stasi's disappearance, twenty-seven-year-old **Catherine Frances**

Clampitt was hired to work at Equi II. Since she was from Wichita Falls, Texas, and had only recently moved to Kansas City in search of work, John Robinson temporarily set her up at a hotel near the company offices. Catherine left her hotel on June 15th of that year to meet with John. She was never seen again.

Between 1987 and 1993, John was in prison for multiple fraud convictions, serving his time in Kansas and Missouri. While at the Western Missouri Correctional Facility, he met 49-year-old **Beverly Bonner**, the prison librarian. The two became close, and upon John's release in 1994, she left her husband and moved to Kansas with him to work for one of his companies.

After John arranged to have Beverly's alimony checks forwarded to a Kansas post office box, she disappeared. For several years, John continued receiving and cashing those checks. He also was still married and living with Nancy Jo and his family.

John began using online chat rooms under the pseudonym "Slavemaster." He used these chat rooms to find women who enjoyed being the submissive partner during role-play sex.

One woman he became acquainted with was 45-year-old **Sheila Faith**. Sheila had a 15-year-old daughter named **Debbie Faith,** who used a wheelchair, and, under the guise of being a wealthy businessman, John offered to pay for Debbie's medical expenses if her mother would accept a job at his company.

In late 1994, Sheila and Debbie left their home in Fullerton, California, and moved to Kansas City. John had Sheila's disability allowance check set up in an account he controlled. Sheila and her daughter Debbie disappeared almost immediately, moving to Kansas City, and John continued to cash Sheila's checks for the next seven years.

Five years later, John became close to another woman he met in a BDSM chat room, 21-year-old Polish immigrant **Izabela Lewicka**. At the time, Izabela was living in Indiana but agreed to move to Kansas City when John professed his love for her. Once together in person, he proposed to her despite still being married to and living with his wife, Nancy, who had no idea he was engaging in such activities on the side. He paid for a marriage license for the pair but never picked it up. It's unclear if Izabela knew she and John weren't legally married.

Lewicka's disappearance wasn't immediate. She lived in an apartment funded by Robinson using an Equi-II credit card. She enrolled in a local community college and adopted the name Izabela Lewicka Robinson. She wore a wedding ring.

Not long after this, she signed a 115-item slave contract, which gave John almost total control over every aspect of her life, including her bank accounts. According to

the slave contract, her only form of written communication with her friends and family could be through e-
mail. In 1999, Lewicka informed her friends about a
forthcoming trip with Robinson. Following that trip, no
one ever physically saw her again, but her family kept
receiving e-mails from her e-mail address.

THE MURDERS CONTINUE

In March of 2000, 27-year-old nurse **Suzette Trouten**
moved from Michigan to Kansas with her two Pekingese
dogs after meeting John Robinson in a BDSM chat
room.

Robinson had offered her a job that involved caring for
John's elderly father and accompanying him on global
travels aboard his yacht. This job was a fabrication, as his
father had died several years earlier and never owned a
yacht.

When Trouten arrived in Kansas, she was placed in a
motel, but her dogs were placed in a kennel because of
the motel's no-pet policy. She initially performed tasks
in John's office and, like Izabela Lewicka, signed a slave
agreement. She also signed several blank sheets of paper.
John told her that some places she would travel would
prevent her from sending mail.

On March 1st, 2000, the day they were scheduled to
embark on their trip to meet his father, John checked

Trouten out of the motel and retrieved her dogs from the kennel. Trouten's communication with her family ceased, and shortly after, two Pekingese dogs were found abandoned near John Robinson's residence.

Trouten's mother contacted John, who falsely claimed that Trouten had found another man, and left. Trouten's mother also received typewritten letters from her daughter, supposedly mailed from abroad, although the envelopes had Kansas City postmarks. She filed a missing person report with the Lenexa police. The police actively investigated and discovered John's history of associations with missing women.

Two women filed sexual battery claims against him in June 2000. The women claimed he had promised them employment and international travel, but when they met him, he sexually assaulted them. One woman claimed he had stolen hundreds of dollars of sex toys from her house. This led to John Robinson's arrest. The police got search warrants for his primary residence, a storage unit, and some farm property to look for the stolen items. What they found, however, was bodies.

On the farm, authorities discovered two 55-gallon drums, each containing the remains of a woman in a highly decomposed state. The victims were later identified as Suzette Trouten and Izabela Lewicka. The medical examiner said both women died from head injuries inflicted by a small, blunt instrument, likely a hammer.

John Robinson's storage unit yielded an additional three barrels, where they found the bodies of Beverly Bonner, Sheila Faith, and her daughter, Debbie Faith. All of the victims had head trauma with a blunt object listed as their cause of death.

KANSAS TRIAL IN 2003

In what became the longest trial in the state's history, John was found guilty of the murders of Trouten, Lewicka, and Stasi, along with fraud, forgery, kidnapping, and interfering with parental custody regarding the abduction of four-year-old Tiffany Stasi.

He received death sentences for the murders of Trouten and Lewicka. Since Stasi's murder occurred before the reinstatement of the death penalty in Kansas, he was sentenced to life imprisonment for her death.

MISSOURI TRIAL

John was tried in Missouri for additional murders, including those of Godfrey, Clampitt, Bonner, and the Faiths. To avoid the death penalty, he entered a guilty plea. He was sentenced to life imprisonment without parole.

In 2005, his wife Nancy filed for divorce after forty-one years of marriage, citing incompatibility and irreconcilable differences as her reasons for doing so.

In 2015, the Kansas Supreme Court overturned the Trouten and Stasi murder convictions on procedural grounds but maintained the conviction and accompanying death sentence for Lewicka's murder.

John Robinson continues to be incarcerated on death row at the El Dorado Correctional Facility in Kansas.

The remains of Paula Godfrey, Lisa Stasi, and Catherine Clampitt have yet to be recovered.

CONFESSIONS

In November 1988, a serial killer, accompanied by his brother, walked into the Humboldt County Sheriff's Office and asked to speak with a police officer. He calmly told the officer that he'd killed four women over the last several years. The man said God had told him to confess because he was feeling "bad." He had evidence with him to prove his story. He pulled a Ziploc bag from his coat pocket and handed it to the officer, who, after a moment, realized it was a severed human breast. He claimed it was from a woman he killed 12 days earlier. His brother knew something was wrong but was shocked at the confession. The man was promptly arrested.

~

Wayne Adam Ford was born to Calvin and Birgette Ford on December 3rd, 1961, in Petaluma, California. The marriage between Wayne's parents was tumultuous, ending in divorce when Wayne was 10, and his brother Rod was 12. Post-divorce, the boys stayed with their father while their mother went off to travel abroad.

In November 1980, Wayne sustained head trauma after being struck by a drunk driver. This was his second head injury after a fall at the age of two. Initially, the childhood incident seemed minor, but the cumulative effect of both events became apparent when Wayne began exhibiting subtle personality and behavioral changes. His relationship with his father deteriorated over frequent arguments, and Wayne left high school to join the Marine Corps in 1988.

A NIGHTMARE MARRIAGE

Kelly Pletcher met Wayne as a teenager in the 1980s. She was drawn to him and loved that he was in the Marine Corps. He was quiet and polite, and she was in love. Wayne proposed, and she accepted. They eloped because Kelly's parents didn't want her to marry him.

Once married, their relationship dynamic changed. Wayne's behavior grew aggressive, and Kelly's self-assurance waned. She chose not to tell her parents about her marital issues, fearing their disapproval yet again. Kelly considered leaving Wayne but felt trapped due to her lack of financial resources. She was a stay-at-home military wife with no job. Wayne knew she was unhappy and threatened to kill her if she attempted to leave.

When Kelly became pregnant, Wayne demanded that she get an abortion. At the clinic, when questioned if she was being coerced, Kelly hesitated. She was informed that the procedure would not proceed if she was being forced. Fearing the consequences in her home life, she eventually said she wasn't being forced and had the abortion.

Wayne's sexual demands escalated into bondage, and he coerced her into odd acts, such as creating wax molds of her breasts. He also insisted that she remain unclothed at home.

He once bought an embarrassingly tiny bikini for her to wear when they went to a pool party with his other Marine buddies. Wayne wanted to show her off. It was a garment that she never would have bought for herself. Kelly felt devalued. She realized Wayne viewed women as objects, valuing them solely for their physical attributes.

Wayne's abuse escalated beyond the confines of their home. He was involved in the alleged sexual assault of two underage girls during a trip to Big Bear alongside one of his friends. After the incident, he sought Kelly's help to evade law enforcement. Despite the severity of the crime, the charges against him were eventually dropped.

Kelly found a job she hoped to use to buy her some time away from Wayne and eventually buy her freedom. She eventually moved out of their home, but Wayne stalked her. He would harass her with phone calls at work, boasting that he knew her every move. On one occasion, he left a chilling message in the dust on her car, writing, "I see you." Kelly lived in constant fear, but she eventually filed for divorce and put distance between herself and Wayne.

~

Now divorced and out of the military with a medical discharge for mental health issues, Wayne's troubles continued in civilian life. He was involved in the assault and robbery of a sex worker. His volatile emotional state led to an arrest and a guilty plea for animal cruelty after he shot and killed a dog in his backyard. His brief incarceration did little to change his violent tendencies.

Now 33, Wayne entered into a new marriage with a 19-year-old woman named Elizabeth, whom he'd met at a karaoke bar. This marriage, like the last, was marred by Wayne's abusive and controlling behavior. In 1995, during an argument while his wife was pregnant, he sexually assaulted her. Elizabeth left him, filed for divorce, and relocated to Las Vegas. Wayne was subsequently denied any visitation rights with his child.

Wayne's response to the divorce was marked by an increase in alcohol abuse, which briefly led to homelessness. He eventually moved in with his grandmother before moving into a trailer in Arcata, California.

Wayne started work as a long-haul truck driver in 1997.

THE FIRST MURDER VICTIM

Wayne Ford's first murder victim, identified as only a
Jane Doe, was found by a duck hunter as he canoed on
the Ryan Slough waterway near Eureka, in Humboldt
County. Her badly mutilated torso was lying on a muddy
bank; her head and limbs were missing, as well as both
breasts, which had been cut off. The hunter immediately
notified the police, but they could not identify the young
woman.

Despite the police having access to her DNA and
conducting routine searches in databases, it would be
decades before she was identified.

On June 7th, 2023, the police, in collaboration with
Othram Laboratory, were finally able to identify the
woman using genetic genealogy. The victim, Kerry Ann
Cummings' remains were claimed and put to rest by her
family.

Kerry's family said she had suffered from mental illness
and had initially left her home in 1997 at the age of 25 to
stay with friends in Eugene, Oregon. Over time, her
family lost communication with her. They filed a
missing person's report and hired a private investigator
to help, but they could not locate her.

TINA GIBBS

In February 1998, Wayne picked up his second victim in his truck. Tina Gibbs, age 26, was from Tacoma, Washington, but she worked as a sex worker in Las Vegas. Tina's naked body was discovered in the California Aqueduct, close to a city named Buttonwillow. The medical examiner determined she died from strangulation and was sexually assaulted and murdered several days before her body was discovered.

LANETTE WHITE

Four months later, Wayne picked up his next victim, Lanette White, 25, at an Ontario truck stop. White's naked body was found in an irrigation canal near Lodi in San Joaquin County. Investigators believed she had been murdered in a different location, and her body was thrown from a moving vehicle into the canal.

PATRICIA TAMEZ

One month after the murder of Lanette, Wayne picked up Patricia Tamaz, 29, from Victorville, at a convenience store. Her body was found floating in the California Aqueduct, close to Hesperia. It had been mutilated, and one breast was missing.

ROD FORD

On November 2nd, 1998, Wayne spent the day drinking. He called his brother Rod from a pay phone in Trinidad, California. Wayne was crying on the phone and asked his brother to meet him so he could tell him something important.

When Rod arrived the following day, Wayne was nervous and anxious. After several hours of discussion, he got Wayne to admit he had hurt some people. Wayne wouldn't say who he hurt or what he did to them, but he told Rod why he hurt them. He was angry with his ex-wife for keeping his child from him.

Rod convinced Wayne that it was important to get help and suggested they go to the police. Once they arrived, Wayne tearfully told the police that he was sorry that he had murdered some people. At this point, he still had the breast of Patricia Tamez in a bag in his pocket. Investigators were able to locate other parts of the bodies that Wayne had saved in a freezer. They never found Kerry Ann Cummings's head or her arms, even though Wayne told them where he hid them.

Wayne confessed to the murders of the four women and was charged with four counts of first-degree murder. His bail was set for $1 million.

In his confessions, Wayne told the officers that he turned himself in because he was afraid his ex-wife in Las Vegas would soon be one of his victims. He also said that he had tried to revive Tina Gibbs by doing CPR on her after he strangled her.

THE LEGAL BATTLE

The legal battle to convict Ford took eight years. Ford claimed he was initially denied a lawyer. His lawyer fought to have his confessions revoked. The prosecutor on the case said that the confessions were legally obtained and that Ford initially asked for an attorney but later changed his mind.

In January 2004, Judge Michael Smith ruled that most of Wayne's confessions were admissible at trial. Yet, those made after November 5th, 1998, three days after Wayne turned himself in, could not be used by the prosecution because the police should have allowed him legal counsel by then.

The defense argued that Ford felt abandoned by his parents and robbed of time with his son. They asked the jury to consider Wayne's mental health and personality disorders, which they claimed didn't allow him to understand the implications of his actions completely.

After a lengthy trial, Wayne was convicted of four counts of first-degree murder on August 1st, 2006. The seven-man, five-woman jury deliberated for more than a week. Wayne Ford was given the death penalty and placed in solitary confinement in San Quentin Prison.

Allegedly, Ford told family and friends he preferred the death penalty.

RECENT YEARS

Wayne Ford is on Death Row at San Quentin Prison and has participated in several podcast interviews. In July 2020, a private investigator and forensic psychology practitioner, Laura Brand interviewed Wayne. Throughout the interview, Wayne's demeanor was unsettling — his laughter and sarcastic tone are particularly jarring as he recounts how the authorities couldn't locate his first victim's head despite him telling them where it was located. He disturbingly jokes about his reaction to receiving the death sentence, saying with a chuckle, "I thought I should have killed more people."

In a November 2023 podcast hosted by Keith Rovere, Ford discusses his interactions with Keith Hunter Jesperson, nicknamed the *Happy Face Killer.* Ford describes how Jesperson suggested creating a feigned interstate dispute as a ploy for Wayne to be transferred to the more comfortable Oregon State Penitentiary. He also revealed to Keith Rovere that he had already decided to turn himself in; he just wanted to spend one final day with his brother.

MICHIGAN MURDERER

JULY 1967 YPSILANTI, MICHIGAN

Daylight was fading as 19-year-old Mary Terese Fleszar left Eastern Michigan University's library and headed home. She carried textbooks under her arm and walked along the quiet street toward her apartment.

A blue-gray Chevrolet drove slowly behind her. The car drew closer, aligning itself with Mary's pace, and the driver, a young man, cranked down the window with a smooth motion. "Hey there! Can I offer you a ride somewhere?"

Mary glanced toward the car, her eyes meeting his for a moment. She replied, "No, thank you. I'm just heading home. It's not far."

Undeterred, the Chevrolet crept alongside her, and the driver tried again. "Come on, it's getting late. I don't mind helping out."

Mary looked at the handsome young man again but shook her head. "Really, I'm okay. Thanks." She was close enough to see her apartment building now and quickened her pace.

THE NEIGHBOR

From a slightly opened window on the fourth floor of Mary's apartment building, her neighbor saw her talking to the man in the Chevrolet and witnessed her shake her head in refusal. They were too far away for her to hear their conversation.

The car stopped, idled for a few moments, and eventually accelerated past Mary, who continued her walk home. The neighbor turned away from the window, not realizing the car had made a U-turn and was headed back toward Mary. She never saw her neighbor enter the building and thought nothing of the incident until Mary was reported missing several days later.

Nearly a month later, on August 7th, Mary Fleszar's decomposed remains were discovered by two teenagers on an abandoned farm in Superior Township. Due to the advanced state of decomposition, dental records were necessary to confirm her identity.

The state of Mary's body hindered the murder investigation, but the cause of her death was unmistakable. She had been brutally stabbed thirty times in the chest and abdomen. Her feet, one hand, and parts of her fingers had been removed.

Two days after Mary's body was found, a man with a camera appeared at the funeral home requesting to photograph Mary's body as a keepsake for her parents. After being denied by the funeral director, he said, "You mean you can't fix her up enough so I could just get one picture of her?" Denied again, he left and drove away in his blue-gray Chevrolet. The director called the police and reported the incident, describing the man and his car in detail. The police didn't follow up on this tip until much later after several more women had been murdered.

～

John Norman Collins was born in Windsor, Ontario, Canada, on June 17th, 1947. He didn't stay there long, as his mother moved across the border to Center Line, a Detroit suburb, to escape an abusive partner. His father's last name was Chapman, but he took the last name Collins as it was the last name of his mother's new husband in Center Line. Collins grew up without knowing his birth father.

Collins was known as a charismatic young man. He was popular in high school, especially with girls, due to his height, good looks, and status as a star pitcher on the baseball team. He did some modeling, entered local bodybuilding competitions, and appeared in magazines. However, he had a darker side. One of his girlfriends later described him as "mad all the time" and sexually aggressive. Another woman said he threatened to kill her during sexual intercourse.

ANOTHER MURDER

Collins continued to kill, and his next victim was Joan Elspeth Schell, a 20-year-old art student from Ann Arbor. Construction workers discovered her body on June 5th, 1968. She had been sexually assaulted and was stabbed 25 times by a four-inch knife. Her throat had been slashed, and her miniskirt was used to strangle her. There was no blood beneath her body, leading investigators to think she had been murdered elsewhere and then dumped at the construction site.

The police noticed the similarities between Mary Fleszar's murder and Joan Schell's. Schell was last seen getting into a car driven by a clean-cut, dark-haired white man, later identified as John Collins. So, the police brought him in for an interview.

Collins denied knowing Fleszar or Schell and claimed to have been with his mother in Center Line during Schell's murder. The police took him at his word and did not verify his alibi.

Collins now felt he could get away with murder easily, and he took the opportunity to kill again.

MARALYNN SKELTON

The body of Maralynn Skelton was found by a property surveyor behind a vacant house on a remote section of Earhart Road in Ann Arbor. She was a 16-year-old Romulus High School student.

One investigator at the scene described Maralynn's injuries as being the worst he had ever seen in thirty years of police work. Before dying, Skelton had been beaten and tortured. A piece of her own shirt was pushed down into her throat to muffle her screams. She had numerous skull fractures and several deep lacerations believed to have been inflicted with a leather strap, and a tree branch had been inserted into her vagina.

The media coverage from the *Ludington Daily News* was unsympathetic in their coverage of Maralynn's death. This is an excerpt from their March 27th, 1969 article.

Latest Ann Arbor Victim Was Caught On Drugs At 13

"Maralynn Skelton, 16, according to police, was a drug user since she was 13, a high school dropout; and a teen-age tripper on LSD, heroin, cocaine, mescaline and amphetamines.

Maralynn Skelton, 16, according to her family, underwent a personality change last fall, became more distant, had hippie friends and was frequently in debt. Her mother said she had no knowledge that her daughter used drugs and gave her $30 last Saturday to pay off her debts.

Maralynn Skelton was found brutally murdered and sexually abused in a wooded area north of here, the fourth such murder of a young girl in two years and the second in a week. Police searched without success for a solution to the killings by unraveling the skein of the brief and eventful life of Maralynn Skelton.

'She tried it all,' said policewoman Mrs. Beverly Scannell, who met Miss Skelton at the request of Romulus High School officials. 'Pep pills one day, heroin the next. The combination was overwhelming. She seemed to get her greatest bang out of LSD,' said Mrs. Scannell, who is attached to the Wayne County sheriff's office."

THE TASK FORCE

Not realizing they had already interviewed their murderer, investigators set up a task force designed to catch the killer before he could strike again. With their eyewitness descriptions and forensic reports, they were able to determine that the same person carried out the three murders. One common thread was the brutal stabbings that occurred in most of the murders. Many of the girls also had shoes and one earring missing as well. They knew their killer was taking keepsakes.

On April 16th, the body of 13-year-old **Dawn Louise Basom** was found on a remote road in Ypsilanti, clad only in a white blouse with her bra wrapped tightly around her neck, marking her as yet another victim of a serial attacker. Dawn had been repeatedly stabbed, and a handkerchief was found in her mouth, presumably to silence her. There was no evidence of sexual assault.

Two months later, on June 9th, 21-year-old University of Michigan graduate **Alice Elizabeth Kalom's** body was found by teenagers in an abandoned farmhouse on North Territorial Road, with a fatal gunshot wound to her forehead. Differing from other cases, there was evidence of sexual assault on Kalom.

The unsolved murders led to public alarm, and the media labeled the perpetrator as the *Michigan Murderer* and the *Co-Ed Killer,* prompting many local women to carry knives and travel in groups for safety.

Nonetheless, on July 26th, Eastern Michigan University student 18-year-old **Karen Sue Beineman** was found nude, severely beaten, and strangled to death. She had been sexually assaulted.

Beineman, a student at Eastern Michigan University, went missing on July 23rd, 1969, and her absence was reported when she didn't return to her dormitory. She was last seen heading to a downtown wig shop before noon. Her body was found three days later in a wooded area near Huron River Parkway.

The police were able to collect a semen sample from Beineman's underwear which had been removed and inserted into her vagina. Oddly, a clipping of blonde hair was stuck to the underwear, yet Beineman was a brunette. Police realized that this hair may be a clue to the place where the murderer was killing his victims before dumping them.

After questioning Beineman's friends and the wig shop owner, they found out that she was seen with a young man on a motorcycle at the wig shop before her death — a man matching the description of John Collins.

The police didn't arrest Collins right away. They talked to his acquaintances and former girlfriends, where they learned about his disturbing history of sexual violence on dates. His male friends said he seemed to derive a perverse pleasure from recounting the gruesome details of the *Michigan Murderer's* crimes to his colleagues, eagerly discussing the injuries inflicted upon each victim when a new case was reported in the newspaper.

THE MISTAKE

In defiance of an explicit directive from the Washtenaw County Prosecutor, two Ann Arbor detectives approached Collins at the Emmet Street apartment he shared with his roommate. They confronted him with the circumstantial evidence against him. Collins maintained his innocence during this encounter, challenging the accuracy of the eyewitnesses who had identified him as the man on the motorcycle with Karen Sue Beineman. He declined an invitation to undergo a polygraph test at the police station. The detectives had not obtained a search warrant for the apartment that day, and no search was conducted. This procedural misstep, breaching the prosecutor's order, signaled to Collins that he was a suspect in all of the murders.

The police would find out later that Collins' roommate witnessed him removing a large box from the apartment shortly after the police left. According to the roommate, the box, partially covered by a blanket, had some women's jewelry, a woman's shoe, rolled-up jean material, and a burlap purse. The roommate also told investigators that Collins had been staying at his uncle's home to feed his German Shepherd while the family was on vacation.

Collins' uncle was State Police Sergeant David Leik, and when he returned from vacation, he was notified that his nephew was a suspect in several murders.

After Sergeant Leik's wife reported some missing items from their basement, like bleach, the basement became the focus of the investigations. Forensic experts initially mistook varnish stains for blood underneath some black paint in the basement. However, an investigator found numerous short blonde hair clippings near the washing machine. Leik explained that his wife cut their children's hair there before their vacation. Additionally, small bloodstains were found in nine areas of the basement, two of which matched Karen Sue Beineman's blood type A.

Forensic neutron analysis compared the blonde hair cuttings found in Beineman's underwear to those found in Leik's basement, confirming a match. Karen Sue Beineman had been in the Leik's basement, and now police had the physical evidence they needed to arrest Collins for the murder of Beineman.

A SWIFT TRIAL

The legal process moved swiftly, and Collins' trial commenced on June 2nd, 1970. By August 19th, John Norman Collins was found guilty of the murder of Karen Sue Beineman. Although definitive evidence linking him to the other murders was lacking, the consensus among law enforcement was that he was also responsible for those additional crimes.

Collins was sentenced to life imprisonment without the possibility of parole, to be served in solitary confinement at Southern Michigan Prison. Despite numerous appeals, his conviction has stood, and he remains incarcerated to this day.

After his conviction, John Norman Collins changed his name to his father's name and is now referred to as *John Chapman*.

His time in prison was troubled; he was found dealing in contraband and planning escapes, one hindered by his broken foot and another foiled escape attempt in 1979, which led to a transfer to a higher security cell block.

Chapman, asserting his dual citizenship, sought a transfer to a Canadian prison in 1981, hoping for an earlier parole. The initial approval was met with public outcry and reversed.

Chapman continues to serve his life sentence, now at G. Robert Cotton Correctional Facility in Jackson, Michigan, where he corresponds with many people, particularly women.

Authors's note: Michigan law student Jane Louise Mixer posted a notice on a college bulletin board looking for someone to drive her across the state to her hometown in Muskegon. The police found her body five days later atop a grave in a cemetery with a raincoat covering her body. A copy of the book *Catch-22* lay beside her. For decades, John Chapman was suspected of this murder even though there were few similarities in the way the crime was perpetrated. In 2005, a man named Gary Earl Leiterman was charged and convicted of Mixer's murder based on DNA evidence.

HOMICIDAL COUSINS

In 1977, Catherine Lorre, daughter of the famed film actor Peter Lorre, was walking in downtown Los Angeles when she was approached by Angelo Buono and Kenneth Bianchi. Initially, they offered her a ride home, not recognizing her as anyone but a young woman alone at night — a woman whom they intended to sexually assault and force into prostitution.

Once they learned her father's identity, the two men, who happened to be fans of Peter Lorre's work in films like *Casablanca* and *The Maltese Falcon*, changed their minds about their initial intentions. This sudden recognition spared Catherine from becoming a victim, as Angelo and Kenneth were collectively *The Hillside Stranglers* responsible for the deaths of ten other women during their killing spree.

Catherine returned home, unaware of the danger she

had just avoided until years later when the men were caught.

~

A HISTORY OF SEXUAL VIOLENCE

Angelo Anthony Buono Jr. was born on October 5th, 1934, in Rochester, New York, to a pair of first-generation Italian-American immigrants from San Buono, Italy. Angelo spent much of his youth getting into trouble, with this escalating to the point that by the time he reached adulthood, he was being arrested for crimes such as grand theft auto and sexual assault.

The degradation and sexual assault of women was a priority for Angelo. Even as a 14-year-old, he boasted to his friends about his desire to "rape women" despite being a self-proclaimed *ladies' man*. He hated women and wanted to both humiliate and injure them when he could.

He did find at least one woman who loved him early on, Geraldine Vinal. The two met in high school and were married in 1955. Less than a week later, he had grown bored with her and left her. They had one child together before their marriage, but Angelo refused to pay child support or even let the boy call him dad going forward.

In 1957, he convinced another woman, Mary Castillo, to

marry him. The pair had five children together before Mary filed for divorce in 1964 over what she described as her husband's violent manner and perverse sexual needs. Once they were separated, he again refused to pay any child support or have any further contact with his children.

He married once more after that, though his aggression made that union short-lived, too.

ANGELO AND KENNY

In 1971, Angelo met another woman and, while in a relationship with her, started sexually abusing her 14-year-old daughter. By 1975, he was alone again. This was when he met his younger cousin, Kenneth "Kenny" Bianchi.

Kenneth was impressed with his older cousin and his ability to get women. Angelo quickly grew close to Kenneth and soon convinced him to join him in his sexual endeavors, such as cruising the streets for sex workers. Both men were short of money, and the pair realized they should recruit some girls to work for them directly, as it would allow them to have the girls and the money they earned, too.

Two teenage runaways, Sabra Hannan and Becky Spears, soon became these recruited sex workers. Once under the control of Angelo and Kenneth and imprisoned in a bedroom, they were forced to sell themselves or be severely beaten.

Sabra and Becky would eventually escape, causing Angelo and Kenneth to look for more vulnerable teenage girls they could force into prostitution. The men spent the money they made as fast as it was coming in, and with the loss of their income, Angelo's Cadillac was briefly repossessed. Desperate for cash, they were now on the prowl for new "sex slaves" on the night they met Peter Lorre's daughter, Catherine.

THE FIRST MURDER

They brought a "trick list" with names of men who frequented certain prostitutes from two sex workers named Deborah Noble and Yolanda Washington, a 19-year-old single mother. When Angelo found out this list was fake, they went to find Debra Noble and kill her. Unable to find her, they located Yolanda Washington on Sunset Boulevard. Both men sexually assaulted her and murdered her, and they dumped her body on a hillside near the Ventura freeway on October 17th, 1977.

Detective Frank Salerno from the LAPD made a statement after the body was found, saying that the killer had washed the body, so little evidence remained other than the bruising confirming the victim was strangled.

After developing a taste for murder, they began cruising

around Los Angeles using fake police badges to lure women into Angelo's Cadillac. Once they'd done so, they'd drive over to Angelo's house, where they'd torture and then murder their victims, eventually dumping them in random locations. Sometimes, they were found in the gulleys of freeway off-ramps on the Golden State Freeway; others were found on a hillside near Dodger Stadium. Their methods of murder changed and grew more complicated. They started with simple strangulation but eventually murdered their victims by lethal injection, electric shock, and carbon monoxide poisoning.

On November 20th, 1977, the body of honors student Kristina Weckler, 20, was found under a bush on a hillside in Los Angeles. She had ligature marks on her neck, wrists, and ankles. There were two puncture marks on her arm, and the medical examiner determined she had had cleaning fluids injected into her body.

One victim was Cindy Hudspeth, a 20-year-old waitress who was murdered on February 17th, 1978. Her remains were found in the trunk of her orange Datsun, a car she had recently purchased with her own money. Her coworker Wanda Huff described Hudspeth as shy but proud of herself for having her own apartment and car. Hudspeth had been strangled and had ligature marks on her body from being restrained before she died.

HILLSIDE STRANGLER TASKFORCE

LAPD officers now had 13 murders on their hands, and they could tie 10 of them to the same person now being called "The Hillside Strangler" in the *Los Angeles Times*. The city of Los Angeles and LA County were offering rewards of up to $125,000 for tips leading to the capture of the killer.

Officer Salerno, now on the task force, spoke to the media about the murders, saying to the *Associated Press*, "You got 20 investigators, you got 20 theories…At this point, we have no tangible leads."

Police Chief Daryl Gates, who was running the task force, said, "I'm embarrassed every time I look at myself in the mirror."

Commander William Booth, who was the spokesman for the police, tried to clean up the officers' statements by saying that Chief Gates does believe the cases will be solved, "He does. I do, and the other investigators do, too."

BIANCHI'S SECRETS

During the time the murders were being committed, Kenneth Bianchi applied for a job within the Los Angeles Police Department and was even taken on several ride-a-longs with officers while they were searching the area for the "Hillside Strangler." Kenneth kept that fact secret from his cousin Angelo.

Angelo and Kenneth attempted to kill another woman, but this would-be victim got away from the men. Kenneth decided this would be a good time to tell Angelo that he had been going on ride-a-longs with the LAPD. He also admitted that the police had questioned him regarding one of the murders but let him go. Angelo was enraged and threatened to kill Kenneth. He said he had to leave the state and knew a place Kenneth could stay in Bellingham, Washington. Angelo gave Kenneth an ultimatum: either leave or die.

Kenneth moved to Bellingham, where he killed two more women. He got a job as a security guard for a house and invited Karen Mandic and Diane Wilder over in 1979. He murdered both of the women in the basement on the same night, and he was arrested the next day.

The police had physical evidence that linked him to Diane's murder. They discovered Diane's hair in the basement of the house. Kenneth's pubic hair was located on Diane's body and in the stairwell to the basement. Diane's menstrual blood was detected on Kenneth's underwear. Both Karen and Diane had been strangled to death, similar to other victims in California.

Initially, Kenneth Bianchi attempted to claim insanity as a defense. During his trial, Bianchi blamed an alternate personality named "Steve Walker" committed the crimes. Kenneth managed to persuade several psychiatrists that he had dissociative identity disorder (previously known as multiple personality disorder.) The prosecution's expert witness said that in actual cases of this disorder, there are usually three or more distinct personalities. In response, Bianchi hastily invented a new identity, "Billy," to support his claim. The court rejected this insanity plea, and Bianchi eventually admitted to faking the multiple personality disorder. He instead agreed to testify against Angelo in exchange for leniency.

His testimony helped to convict Angelo Buono, though not before he underwent the longest trial in American legal history at the time. The trial lasted from November 1981 to November 1983, at which point Angelo was found guilty on nine counts of murder and sentenced to life imprisonment. Ronald M. George, the judge tasked with overseeing the trial, later commented that he felt the death sentence would have been a more appropriate punishment in hindsight if the jury had allowed it.

Kenneth Bianchi would meet a similar fate, being sentenced to life imprisonment without the possibility of parole. He is currently in the Washington State Penitentiary in Walla Walla, Washington.

INCARCERATED LIFE

In 1986, while in Calipatria State Prison, Angelo married

Christine Kizuka, a mother of three and supervisor at the California State Employment Development Department. Almost two decades after that, in September of 2002, he died of a heart attack. His body was later cremated.

In 2007, his dark legacy carried on when grandson Christopher Buono also became a murderer after shooting his grandmother Mary Castillo in the head. Once he was finished doing this, he then turned his gun on himself. At the time of his death, he had only recently become aware of his grandfather's true identity and his family's overall legacy.

Author's Note: Please see Appendix B for a complete list of the victims.

THE VAN

On June 26th, 1978, Sandra Kaye Butler, 16, called her mother at work and asked if she could ride her bike from her Sparks, Nevada, home to the Reno Rodeo at the nearby Washoe County Fairgrounds. Her mother agreed so the young girl started her journey in the early afternoon. Her first stop was the Greenbrae Shopping Center across the street from her apartment building. A neighbor remembered seeing her there; this was the last time Sandra was seen alive.

To her family's dismay, the police classified her as a runaway and took minimal action to try and find her in those first critical days.

Sandra's body was never found, and it's a widely accepted theory that she was the first victim of a string of sexual assaults and murders carried out by Gerald and Charlene Gallego.

It has never been confirmed if Gerald and Charlene took Sandra Kaye Butler on the day she went missing, but it has been confirmed that they were at the Reno Rodeo on the day Sandra asked her mother if she could go.

~

Gerald Gallego was born in Sacramento, California, on July 17th, 1946. Family life was difficult for him growing up as his father was a career criminal who was rarely home. His father, Gerald Gallego Sr., would later be executed in a Mississippi gas chamber for killing a police officer by throwing acid in his face during an attempted prison escape.

Gerald's mother was a sex worker, and this path led her to have many boyfriends, some of whom would beat Gerald for any misbehavior. Despite this, the boy regularly begged for attention but was rarely given it and was usually left hungry, dirty, and fending for himself.

When Gerald was ten, he was arrested for robbing a neighbor's home; this led to twenty-two further arrests, usually involving a burglary or robbery charge, and multiple stints in prison. At age 12, Gerald was sent to a California Youth Authority facility after sexually abusing a six-year-old girl. Gerald married seven times throughout his life, and he had one child, a daughter, Mary Ellen, whom he also sexually abused.

Charlene Gallego (nee Williams) was born in Stockton,

California, on October 10th, 1956. Her father was a successful and well-known businessman who provided well for his family. While Charlene was still a child, her mother was seriously injured in a car accident. Unable to care for her child, Charlene had to accompany her father on his many business trips and had an unstable childhood.

As a young adult, Charlene began experimenting with drugs and alcohol. She also gained a reputation as a "nymphomaniac" among her peers because she was seen as overly flirtatious with men. Eventually, she married a young heroin addict, though this marriage fell apart, partially due to her high sexual demands. The same would happen with her second marriage and future relationships until she met Gerald Gallego.

Gerald and Charlene met at a poker club in Sacramento, California, on September 10th, 1977, and immediately hit it off as both shared sadomasochistic sexual interests. They eventually started living together, and after several months, Gerald brought home a 16-year-old exotic dancer who engaged in a threesome with the pair. Gerald didn't want the two women to touch each other, and when he found out later they had, he beat Charlene and refused to have sex with her again. Gerald admitted that having a willing sexual partner wasn't enough for him. He was only aroused by a sex slave fantasy, and he needed an unwilling partner. In a desperate attempt to keep the relationship alive and satisfy her lover, Charlene agreed to find a pair of sex slaves for Gerald.

1978

Rhona Scheffler, 16, and **Kippi Vaught**, 17, were shopping at the mall in Sacramento, California, on September 10th, 1978, when Charlene tricked the girls into getting into their van.

Throughout the night that followed, the two girls were repeatedly sexually assaulted in the van. The next day, both were killed by Gerald after being struck in the head with a tire iron and then shot at close range. They were buried in a ditch in Sloughhouse, California. Their naked bodies were found by a farmer two days later.

1979

Approximately one year after **Sandra Kay Butler's** disappearance, the Gallegos would kidnap two more teenage girls from the Reno area.

Those girls were **Brenda Judd**, 14, and **Sandra Colley**, 13. Both had been lured into the Gallego's van with the promise of earning money if they helped the couple distribute flyers around the area. After they got in the van and were miles from the Washoe County fairground, Gerald repeatedly sexually assaulted the girls while Charlene drove the van.

At one point, Charlene pulled over and had Gerald watch as she forced the girls to perform sexual acts on one another. After that, Gerald murdered both girls by repeatedly hitting them over the head with a shovel. Once this was done, he dug a large pit with the same shovel and buried them under rocks.

1980

The next victims of the Gallegos would be **Stacey Ann Redican** and **Karen Chipman-Twiggs**, both seventeen years old. On the morning of April 24th, 1980, Gerald woke Charlene and told her to get up and get him a girl. After driving around, the Gallegos noticed Redican and Chipman-Twiggs leaving a bookstore. Charlene approached the two girls and offered them marijuana, which she said they could smoke with her in her van if they wanted.

The two girls accepted, though once they made it to the van, they were held at gunpoint by Gerald as Charlene drove off. The girls were tied up and sexually assaulted numerous times by Gerald. Once he was finished, Charlene parked at a secluded area just outside of Lovelock, Nevada, where the girls were led out into the woods and murdered. Their brutalized bodies were discovered three months later in shallow graves, their hands still tied together with macrame rope.

On June 6th, 1980, in Port Orford, Oregon, **Linda Teresa Aguilar**, 21, became the next victim of the couple. She had been hitchhiking when they picked her up. She was four months pregnant, and she was sexually assaulted and murdered. Gerald hit her head with a rock, then strangled her. He dug a hole in the sand and buried her. Her body was found the next day by a couple walking near the beach. The medical examiner who completed the autopsy found sand in Linda's lungs, which meant Gerald had buried her alive.

One month after that, on July 17th, 31-year-old **Virginia Mochel** was also abducted, this time from a parking lot of a West Sacramento tavern where she worked as a bartender. Gerald and Charlene knew Virginia as they frequented that bar and had even been served by Virginia on multiple occasions. She was bound, sexually assaulted, and strangled with fishing line, and her body was dumped in a pond just outside of Clarksburg.

FINAL VICTIMS

In the early hours of November 2nd, 1980, after a night of drinking at a bar in Sacramento, Gerald told Charlene he had the urge again and wanted to abduct a woman. Now heavily pregnant, Charlene reluctantly complied, driving them in his car to a nearby shopping center. Here, they spotted a young couple getting into a car. Gerald said he wanted them, but Charlene dismissed the idea, pointing out it was a male and female together, and the couple had already started their car, so they moved on. Gerald was now focused on having a male and a female, so they continued looking.

Their attention soon shifted to another couple, 22-year-old **Craig Miller** and his fiancé, 21-year-old **Mary Elizabeth Sowers**, who were also getting into their car after leaving a formal fraternity dance. Gerald told Charlene to pull over; he quickly got out and, at gunpoint, told Craig and Mary to get in the Gallegos's car, a blue Oldsmobile Cutlass.

A friend of Craig's, Andy Beal, recognized the couple getting into the strange car. As he approached the Oldsmobile, Craig quickly told him to leave, saving his friend's life. Charlene shoved Beal and told him to back off. Heeding the warning, Beal left but memorized the car's plate as it drove away and promptly called the police, but it was too late. Craig Miller and Mary Elizabeth Sowers would be the final victims of the Gallegos.

Craig and Mary were driven to a remote location near Bass Lake, California. During the drive, Gerald asked Charlene if she wanted to have Craig Miller. She declined the offer, so Gerald told Charlene to pull over, and he made Craig get out of the car. Gerald shot him in the back of the head and then got in the back seat with a terrified Mary. He put his arm around her and said that tonight, she was going to be his "Mary Ellen," the name of Gerald's daughter whom he'd sexually abused.

Charlene drove back to their apartment, where Gerald drugged Mary and sexually assaulted her most of the night. Once he was done, he told Charlene to drive them to a rural area in Placer County, California, where

Gerald pulled Mary out of the car. He shot her twice in the head and one in the neck, and they left.

Gerald told Charlene that he loved her and that they should have breakfast. The couple went to have coffee and donuts.

The next day, Craig Miller's body was found by two people out for a walk near the lake. His body was lying face down, and he was still wearing his formal suit from the dance. Mary Sowers's badly decomposed body was discovered three weeks later.

The information from Andy Beal allowed authorities to track the Gallegos down several days later at a Western Union office where Charlene's parents were wiring her $500. They were arrested and charged with the kidnapping and murders of Craig Miller and Mary Elizabeth Sowers. Both Gerald and Charlene pleaded not guilty to the charges.

After extensive negotiations, Charlene's legal team persuaded prosecutors across multiple states to agree to a plea bargain in exchange for her testimony against Gerald. Her sentence for changing her plea to guilty was reduced to 16 years and eight months in prison.

DEATH OF AN INMATE

Gerald would receive the death penalty in California for

the murders of Craig Miller and Mary Beth Sowers and, as a result, would be sent to death row. Gallego was extradited to Nevada to stand trial for the murders of Karen Chipman Twiggs and Stacey Redican, whose bodies were found in Lovelock, Nevada. The county didn't have enough money for a trial, so a California newspaper columnist created a public appeal for funds. More than $20,000 came in to fund the trial, and Gerald was found guilty of both murders and given the death penalty. It was the nation's first murder prosecution partially financed by citizens.

On July 18th, 2002, Gerald died of rectal cancer while awaiting execution in Nevada. He was fifty-six years old.

An article in the *San Francisco Chronicle* on July 20th, 2002, read, "Gerald Gallego, the "sex-slave" killer who, with his wife, cut a lethal swath through California and Nevada more than 20 years ago, died of cancer in a Nevada prison hospital Thursday night, cheating the state out of executing him."

1997

Charlene completed her sentence in July of 1997 and was released under the condition that she agreed to register as a sex offender wherever she took up residence.

When she was arrested, Charlene was pregnant. While in

prison, she gave birth to a son but never had custody
of him.

Charlene returned to Sacramento and engaged in
charity work for military families. She changed her last
name back to her maiden name, Williams. Her current
whereabouts are unknown, but it is known she has since
left California.

She claims she never killed anyone despite pleading
guilty to kidnapping and murder. She denied any will-
ingness to be part of the murders, insisting she was
coerced and abused by Gerald and could not stop him
despite her efforts.

Charlene claims she was forced to lure the girls into
their van, where Gerald, armed and waiting, would
initiate their abduction, assault, and murder. Their
murder spree spanned three states, claiming the lives of
10 people and an unborn child.

THE DEATH PENALTY

In 1991, Latvia regained its independence after the fall
of the Soviet Union, a significant milestone that marked
the beginning of a new political era for the Baltic state.
The nation began to reshape its legal system, which
included reevaluating its stance on capital punishment.

Under Soviet rule, the death penalty was reserved for
severe crimes such as murder, and the sole method of
execution remained unchanged: a single bullet to the
back of the head. The last executions in Latvia took
place in January 1996, five years after the country's
liberation from Soviet control.

In October 1996, Latvian President Guntis Ulmanis
declared that he would commute any death sentence to a
term of life imprisonment. Despite this, Latvia
continued to hand down death sentences until 1998. In
February 1999, Latvia formally abolished the death
penalty. However, this landmark decision was soon

followed by a crime that tested the nation's resolve. On February 22, 1999, a mere 18 days after the abolition of the death penalty, a horrifying massacre of small children shocked the country.

～

GULBENE, LATVIA 1999

Alexander Koryakov, age 21, had his hunting knife, two meat cleavers, and some gas spray. His murder kit was now complete. He'd been staking out his prey for almost a week now. Each day, he watched the children come and go from the local kindergarten, listening to them speak and gauging their size and how fast they walked or ran. He wanted to kill the Russian-speaking children. He'd even called the school to see if the Russian children had their own class. They did, and now he knew exactly where the class was.

He had two options: kill the children as they exited the school or kill them in the classroom. His surveillance made him realize how easily adults came and went from the school. Alexander could easily walk in unchallenged. He'd say he was looking for his little brother if he were stopped. He chose to kill the children in the classroom. They would be contained, and he wouldn't have to chase them or fight off parents picking their children up from school.

It was early afternoon on the day of the event, and Alexander struck during nap time. He walked into the school as planned, and no one noticed him or questioned his presence. He went directly to the kindergarten nursery for Russian-speaking children. The children were supposed to be napping, but a small group of young girls were clustered together talking. He viciously attacked them with one of his cleavers, causing screaming, crying, and confusion from the other children. The three girls that quickly succumbed to their injuries were ages three, four, and five. Several children were able to run away when their brave teacher, a 32-year-old woman, attempted to stop Alexander. She was also murdered with the cleaver. The school nurse who ran into the room was attacked by Alexander, but he ran out after hacking at her twice with the cleaver. She was severely injured but survived.

Alexander quickly walked out of the school and along the highway from Gulbene to Riga, the capital city. His shirt was drenched in the blood of his victims. He was out of breath and staggered as he walked, exhilarated from what he had done. A police officer approached him, concerned that Alexander was covered in blood, not knowing what had just happened at the kindergarten. Alexander fell into the policeman's arms, and a few minutes later, once the policeman was informed of the massacre, he was under arrest.

Once arrested, Alexander willingly confessed to his crimes, revealing every detail of his disturbing plan to kill the kindergartners and even his plans to murder other children beyond that. He told the police this act was merely the beginning of a killing spree that would eventually surpass infamous Russian serial killer Andrei Chikatilo's record of murdering 52 women and children.

Andrei Chikatilo, idolized by Alexander, was a notorious Soviet serial killer known as "The Butcher of Rostov." He was convicted for the murders of 52 people, primarily young women and children, from 1978 to 1990. Chikatilo's modus operandi involved luring his victims from transportation hubs to secluded areas with promises of money, alcohol, or candy, where he would then brutally murder them for sexual gratification. His crimes were marked by extreme violence, including mutilation and gouging out the victims' eyes.

Alexander explained to the police that he had read all of the books and magazines available materials on Andrei Chikatilo and that he had spent a year planning the massacre. He had considered killing members of his family to see if he could go through with the murders of the children, but he later decided against this.

The police had several psychiatrists evaluate Alexander, and they concluded he knew what he was doing and was fit to stand trial.

During the trial, Alexander Koryakov testified on his own behalf. The courtroom became an arena where he could recount and relive the murders, which he did without a shred of emotion. He faced the grief-stricken parents and relatives of the victims without remorse. His only regret, he claimed, was his failure to kill more people. He intended to achieve fame through his actions.

"A year ago, I read a book about the worst of American criminals. There have been documented cases of mass murder. All these killers became famous. And then I decided to kill children because it causes the greatest public outcry and their parents more grief. They are easy to kill, they cannot resist physically."

ALEXANDER KORYAKOV

He was found guilty of the murders of the three children and their teacher and sentenced to life in prison.

Latvian President Ulmanis declared the murders as one of the worst acts of violence in Latvian history. He called for new security measures for schools and a better system to protect children.

A BACKYARD BURIAL

On March 9th, 1988, Benjamin Fink, 55, moved into a boarding house in Sacramento, California. By the time April was over, he would be dead.

His landlady told his brother, who had been visiting regularly, that he had left suddenly and had left no forwarding address. His brother found that hard to believe since his brother had mobility problems. The landlady had no further answers for the brother and told him she was too busy working on projects in her back-yard to track down Mr. Fink. Outside, near her metal shed, she was supervising two workers pouring a concrete pad.

The police came to the house and inquired about Mr. Fink. Again, she told them he had left but slightly changed her story. She said Mr. Fink, who was known to abuse alcohol, was a nuisance, so she threw him out of the boarding house.

Seven months later, Benjamin's body was found in a hole just under the concrete pad, which now had a gazebo on top. His body was covered in blue absorbent pads, wrapped in plastic, and secured with duct tape. The toxicology report from the medical examiner revealed the presence of two strong sedatives and an anti-psychotic drug in his body.

～

Dorothea Helen Gray was born in Redlands, California, on January 9th, 1929. Her parents had alcoholism; her mother was a sex worker, and her father was mentally unstable to the point where he would repeatedly threaten to kill himself in front of Dorothea and her siblings. He ultimately died of tuberculosis in 1937, which was followed by his wife's death two years later.

After their parents died, the children were sent to an orphanage, where Dorothea was sexually abused. She escaped this life when she turned sixteen and married Fred McFaul, a soldier who had just returned from the Pacific theater of World War II. They had two daughters together, though the couple would raise neither because she was sent to prison.

In 1948, Dorothea was arrested after she was caught purchasing women's accessories with forged checks. She served four months in prison and was given three years of probation. Fred left her during this time. Upon her release, she moved to San Francisco, where, in 1952, she met and married a merchant seaman named Axel Johan Johansson.

By then, Dorothea had created a new identity, Teya Singoalla Neyaarda, a supposed Muslim woman of Egyptian and Israeli descent. While under this guise, she took advantage of her husband's frequent trips out to sea by inviting men into her home for sex and gambling away his Axel's money.

Dorothea was arrested again in 1960 for owning and operating a bookkeeping firm, which was nothing more than a front for a brothel. She was sentenced to ninety days in prison, and soon after her release, Axel had her committed to DeWitt State Hospital, where doctors diagnosed her as a pathological liar.

Dorothea and Axel divorced in 1966, and she changed her identity again, this time to Sharon Johansson, a devout Christian who allowed young, impoverished, and abused women to live with her without any charge.

She married Roberto Puente, though they would separate and divorce sixteen months later when she claimed he had abused her.

Following their divorce, Dorothea began running a boarding house in Sacramento, where she continued to help those in need and, in the process, created a public persona of being a respectable older woman.

However, in December of 1978, she was convicted of illegally cashing 34 checks that belonged to her tenants. She was given five years of probation and forced to pay $4,000 in restitution. Despite this, her reputation remained solid enough that her boarding house continued to be successful.

On January 16th, 1982, her next known crime occurred when she picked up Malcolm McKenzie, 74, at a bar and took him back to her apartment, where she proceeded to drug him and rob him.

Three months after this, on April 28th, Dorothea committed her first murder. Ruth Monroe, aged 61, was found dead of a codeine overdose just two weeks after moving into Dorothea's boarding house. At the time, her death was considered to be a suicide, and there was no investigation.

A month later, on May 16th, Dorothy Milbourne, 49, found her checkbook and credit card missing. She had visited Dorothea's home a few hours earlier and realized the landlady had taken it. In July of 1982, Dorothea Puente was convicted on two counts of grand theft and sentenced to five years in prison.

PRISON AGAIN

During her time behind bars, she began communicating with Everson Gillmouth, a 77-year-old retiree from

Oregon. In September 1985, Dorothea was released early and was picked up by Everson. They were engaged to be married one month later.

Before their wedding, Dorothea hired a handyman to build her a six-foot by thirty-inch wooden storage box. The day after this job was completed, the handyman returned for payment and found the box nailed shut. Dorothea asked him to help her take it to a location near a river about an hour from Sacramento, where she proceeded to dump it.

On January 1st, 1986, the body of Everson Gillmouth was discovered inside this box, though it would not be identified as him for another 12 years. Dorothea had convinced Everson's family that he was still alive by sending them fake letters and postcards.

In October of 1986, Betty Mae Palmer, 78, moved into Dorothea's boarding house where, soon after, she became a victim. Dorothea killed her, forged an ID in her name, and then began collecting her Social Security checks. The police later discovered part of her body in a hole in Dorothea's front yard. Her head, hands, and legs were never recovered.

That same month, Dorothea summoned a notary to the hospital room of another tenant, 78-year-old Leona Carpenter, after she had undergone an overdose of sleeping tablets. Dorothea was given power of attorney over Leona. Ten days later, she also began cashing

Leona's Social Security checks. Once Leona's health had recovered, she returned to Dorothea's boarding house but disappeared soon after.

In February 1987, James Gallop, 62, moved into Dorothea's boarding house. Five months later, he discovered he had colon cancer. Before he could undergo treatment, Dorothea contacted his doctor's office to say he had left for Los Angeles and wouldn't be returning for the foreseeable future.

The same month James Gallop allegedly left Sacramento, Eugene Gamel, 58, another tenant, was found dead of an apparent suicide. Dorothea told the police he had a history of suicide attempts, though it's unclear if this was accurate.

On October 2nd, 1987, sixty-one-year-old Vera Faye Martin was sent to live with Dorothea Puente at her boarding house. Three days later, the landlady started cashing Vera's Social Security checks. On October 19th, Vera failed to contact her daughter on her birthday. She would never be heard from again.

Two days after this, on October 21st, Dorothy Miller, 65, moved into an upstairs flat at the boarding house. By November, Miller had disappeared, and a carpet cleaner had been hired to remove a large pile of foul-smelling slime from her room. Dorothea would begin cashing her Social Security checks following her disappearance. Her body was later discovered under concrete in the back yard near several rose bushes. Tissue samples from an autopsy on the remains said her brain tissue contained the presence of a sedative and an anti-seizure medication.

The following year, in February, Alvaro Montoya, 51, moved into Dorothea's boarding house. By August, she was telling everyone who knew him that he had gone to Mexico to visit some relatives. While Mr. Montoya Spoke Spanish, his family was from Costa Rica. The Social Security office suspected something was amiss then and even threatened to call the police until a letter was sent to them from Alvaro's "brother-in-law" in Mexico stating that he was okay.

Nine months later, on November 7th, after Benjamin Fink had also gone missing, a former resident of Dorothea's boarding house, John Sharp, spoke to the police about the disappearance of Alvaro Montoya. He claimed Dorothea had something to do with it. Four days later, a detective visited the boarding house and, with her permission, began digging in areas that appeared to have recently been disturbed.

Thirty minutes into the digging, the first body was discovered. While other bodies were being unearthed, Dorothea slipped away. She hopped on a bus to Los Angeles and was later found at an LA motel thanks to a tip from a hotel maintenance person. She was arrested there on November 16th, 1988, for the murder of Alvaro Montoya.

On March 31st, 1989, Dorothea was formally charged with a further eight counts of murder. According to investigators, most of her victims had been drugged until they overdosed. Then, after that, they had been wrapped in bed sheets and plastic lining before being dragged out into the back yard for burial.

~

On February 9th, 1993, Dorothea's trial began. The trial was a high-profile event, partly due to the shocking nature of the crimes and partly because of Dorothea Puente herself, who appeared to be a frail woman incapable of committing murder and burying bodies.

The prosecution presented a largely circumstantial case, as there was little physical evidence directly linking Dorothea to the murders. While bodies had been found buried in her yard, the prosecution had no physical evidence that Dorothea murdered them or buried them. They relied on the testimony of her tenants, who had survived, and the financial records showing her theft of the victim's social security checks.

The testimony of social workers and other witnesses who had interacted with Puente and her tenants painted a picture of Dorothea as a manipulative individual who preyed on vulnerable members of society. These testimonies were crucial in portraying the pattern of behavior that led to the murders.

The defense, on the other hand, attempted to cast doubt on the prosecution's evidence, arguing that the deaths could have been due to natural causes, given the age and health of the victims. Dorothea's defense team pointed out the lack of direct physical evidence tying her to the murders, such as DNA or fingerprints. They presented Dorothea Puente as a caring individual who took in society's outcasts, suggesting that the deaths were unfortunate but not the result of foul play.

On August 2nd of that same year, after hearing the testimony of 156 witnesses, the jury informed the judge that they were deadlocked on all nine counts of murder. Twenty-four days later, this deadlock was finally broken for three counts. Dorothea was convicted of the murders of Benjamin Fink, Leona Carpenter, and Dorothy Miller.

The trial's outcome was a mix of relief for the families, as many felt justice was only partially served. Some saw the conviction on only three counts as a failure to fully hold Dorothea accountable for the extent of her crimes.

On December 10th, Dorothea Puente was sentenced to life imprisonment without the possibility of parole. She was incarcerated at the Central California Women's Facility in Chowchilla, California, where she remained until her death as a result of natural causes on March 27th, 2011, at the age of eighty-two.

In 2004, she also released a cookbook called *Cooking with a Serial Killer,* which contains 60 dishes she served at her boarding house. It is still available to buy from book retailers.

The boarding house she once operated in Sacramento was included in the 2013 home tour held by the Sacramento Old City Association. It has been periodically opened again for tours since then.

The victims of Dorothea Puente:
Victim, age, recorded year of death

- Ruth F. Munroe, 61, 1982
- Everson Theodore Gillmouth, 77, 1986
- Leona Carpenter, 78, 1988
- Benjamin Fink, 55, 1988
- James A. Gallop, 64, 1988
- Vera Faye Martin, 65, 1988
- Dorothy Miller, 65, 1988
- Alvaro "Bert" Montoya, 52, 1988
- Betty Mae Palmer, 80, 1988

REMAINS OF GRIEF

"I was only able to bury the parts of my daughter that the police could find. He cut her up in little pieces and threw them around the city like they were pieces of meat."

JOHN BUNTING JR., VICTIM IMPACT
STATEMENT

In December of 1995, the body of **Kelly Sue Bunting** was discovered wrapped up in a sleeping bag in Melville, New York. Kelly, who also went by the name Melanie, was a 28-year-old sex worker from Queens who had last been seen earlier that month. Some of her remains were found in a Melville trash bin. She had been badly beaten, and her hands had been removed, something her killer had done to impede identification. It wasn't until four months later that the killer was finally caught, and police realized Kelly had been one of five victims of a serial killer whose brother, a postal worker, helped him dispose of the bodies.

~

Robert Yale Shulman was born on March 28th, 1954, in Hicksville, Long Island, New York. Not much is known of his younger years, except that he grew up in both Long Beach and New Jersey and graduated from high school while living in the latter area in 1972. It's also known that after graduating, he took courses at Hofstra University for two years but eventually stopped and began a job as a mail sorter for the post office.

He had a younger brother named Barry, also a postal worker, with whom he appeared to be close. The two remained close throughout their lives, and when Robert started frequenting sex workers and then killing them, Barry, not wanting his brother to go to prison, helped him dismember the women and spread their body parts across New York.

The first victim of Robert's was **Lori Vasquez**, who was 24 years old at the time of her disappearance in the Summer of 1991. Lori was a sex worker from Brooklyn whom Shulman had picked up one night after visiting a popular sex worker hangout in Hollis, Queens. After taking her back to his home in Long Island, he smoked crack cocaine with her and then beat her to death with a baseball bat. Following this, he contacted his brother Barry and informed him of what he'd done.

It's unclear what Barry's initial reaction to this news was, but he ultimately went to Robert's home and helped him cut off the girl's hands. After that, the pair loaded the corpse into Barry's car and drove over to Yonkers, where they dumped it in a garbage can. Lori's body would be found on August 31st of that same year, though it would be a full five years before police figured out who her killer was.

"He has torn up my family completely. She [Lori Vasquez] wanted to change her life, and this gentleman took her life away."

DAWN PAUL, SISTER OF LORI VASQUEZ, VICTIM IMPACT STATEMENT

In the meantime, Robert laid low for a while. Eventually, he returned to killing in the spring of 1995. His next victim was **Lisa Ann Warner**, an 18-year-old sex worker from Jamaica, Queens. She went missing at that time and wouldn't be discovered until April 6th when a worker at a recycling plant in Brooklyn came across her dismembered body on a conveyor belt at the Star Recycling Plant in Williamsburg, Brooklyn.

Lisa had also been picked up by Robert while he was out cruising for prostitutes. Like with his prior victim, he'd taken her back to his home in Long Island and, after smoking crack with her, had beaten her to death and then disposed of her body. It's believed that Barry Shulman once more helped his brother with the body disposal.

Lisa Ann's mother, Ruth Brown, told the media that Lisa Ann had run away from home several times before turning to sex work to support herself.

An unidentified woman, referred to by police as **Yonkers Jane Doe**, had been found dead and dismembered inside a dumpster in Yonkers, New York, on June 27th, 1992. The police were unable to figure out who had killed her, but now they believed it was the same person who had killed Lori Vasquez, Lisa Ann Warner, and Kelly Sue Bunting.

In 2018, Yonkers Police Detective John Geiss told the media, "She was a person that was just dumped like garbage, and we want to give her an identity, be able to tell the family at least we know what happened to her."

It took 30 years, but on Dec. 7th, 2021, Carl Koppelman, a volunteer forensic genealogist for the DNA Doe Project, wrote on his Facebook page that he had the family's permission to share that Yonkers Jane Doe was 31-year-old mother, Meresa Hammond who was living in New Jersey at the time of her disappearance.

Another unidentified woman, named **Medford Jane Doe**, had been found on the shoulder of Long Island Avenue between Yaphank and Medford on December 7th, 1994, by an employee of the Suffolk County Department of Public Works. Like Teresa Hammond, she had been badly beaten and dismembered, leading police to now believe she was a victim of the same killer.

Medford Jane Doe was found inside a brand-new blue Rubbermaid garbage can. Her nude body was partially covered with plastic bags, and she had a white towel wrapped around her head. A white powdery substance, later determined to be baking soda, was visible on the body. Her left leg was severed midway between the knee and groin area, and both arms had been amputated. The victim had blunt force trauma to the face, head, eye, nose, and mouth, according to the medical examiner's report. Her left arm had a tattoo consisting of a red heart and a banner with the name "Adrian."

Hoping to catch the perpetrator before they could strike again, police started canvassing hotels around the areas where the murders had taken place. At one hotel, they were told about a suspicious-looking man cruising around regularly in a blue Cadillac. Investigators eventually used the car's make and model to lead them to a residence in Hicksville where a neighbor had recently seen the vehicle.

The car was registered to Barry Shulman, John's brother, so police moved in to question him. He denied knowing anything about the murders. The sleeping bag Kelly Sue Bunting had been found in was manufactured and sold by Sears department stores. So they contacted Sears to find out if Barry Shulman had purchased a sleeping bag from them with a credit card but were informed he hadn't done so. They did, however, have a record of a Robert Shulman buying a sleeping bag from them recently.

The investigators were now hunting for Robert Schulman. This became an urgent priority when, not long after that, a woman identified Robert Schulman as the man she'd seen driving around the streets in the blue Cadillac. The Cadillac owned by Barry was now in police evidence after an inspection by police cadaver dogs signaled positively for human remains inside the vehicle.

The police found Robert at his place of work on April 6th, 1996. He was arrested and taken back to the station, where, following a brief interrogation, he confessed to the murders of Lori Vasquez, Lisa Ann Warner, and Kelly Sue Bunting. He claimed he hadn't intended to kill them and had only done so in a drug-fueled haze. He argued that after smoking crack cocaine with each of them, he'd blacked out and then woken up again with them already dead.

The local news media questioned neighbors who'd known Robert. Most described him as weird and someone they'd tried to avoid. One neighbor, Henry M.

Bialick, said, "In all the ten or twelve years he lived there, he never once spoke a word to us. We had him pegged as a little weird, but of course, nobody thought he was a killer."

Robert was put on trial for the murder of Kelly Sue Bunting at Suffolk County Court in November of 1998. The prosecution pursued the death penalty, a penalty that had only been reinstated in New York State four years prior. On March 4th, a jury convicted him of first-degree murder. On May 7th, Judge Arthur Pitt sentenced him to death.

On June 3rd, while awaiting trial for the additional murders of Lori Vasquez and Lisa Ann Warner, Robert attempted suicide by trying to cut his wrists with a razor blade. He was found and taken to a prison hospital, where he made a full recovery.

While in prison, Robert also admitted to the murders of the other two victims, Yonkers Jane Doe (Maresa Hammond) and Yonkers Jane Doe. He couldn't help them identify the Jane Does as he said he never knew their names.

Robert's brother Barry was also indicted on charges of hindering the prosecution and unlawfully disposing of dead bodies. He pleaded guilty to these charges and received a two-year sentence behind bars. It is not believed he had any involvement in the actual killings.

The remaining victim, Medford Jane Doe, has yet to be identified as of 2024. John Schulman confessed to her murder, saying that he killed her in his room and blacked out after smoking crack with her. When he woke up, she was dead, so he used a hacksaw to dismember her body. He sprayed her body with air freshener and baking soda to mask the odor.

TAKEN OFF DEATH ROW

In October of 2005, while awaiting execution, Robert was taken off death row. He was re-sentenced to life without the possibility of parole. On April 13th, 2006, Robert died in an Albany hospital. The cause of death remains unclear, but it was believed to be from natural causes.

"Vengeance is mine, sayeth the Lord. Even though man took away the death penalty, he deserved it, and he got it. I feel it's the Almighty's justice system." said Ruth Brown, mother of Lisa Ann Warner.

BLOODY BAYOU

On July 12th, 1997, 19-year-old David Mitchell was walking home from his grandmother's house after attending a family birthday party. Along his journey home, he decided to hitchhike, and a man offered him a ride in his car. The man had a kind smile, blue eyes, and a scraggly red beard. David noticed that the man was obese, and his walking cane lay in the passenger seat. He accepted the ride, and as the man drove along, he told David about his girlfriend and how they liked to have group sex. David accepted the man's proposition for a sexual liaison and went to the man's trailer, where he quickly realized there was no girlfriend.

Two days later, David's body was discovered in a watery ditch along a highway in St. Charles Parish. The medical examiner found water from the ditch in David's lungs and listed his death as accidental drowning. There were no signs of physical trauma on the body, and he had no drugs or alcohol in his system. David's pants were found around his ankles, suggesting something sexual had taken place, but the lack of bruising on the body or signs of a struggle suggested it might have been consensual.

"He told me that he wasn't going anywhere, he was going to wait for his uncle to give him a ride back to Luling. My brother didn't show up, so I guess he decided to try to hitchhike back to his mom's...My sister has never made peace with this death. Her only child is murdered. Every year she buys him Christmas, Birthday, and Easter presents. His pictures are in every room of this house."

MRS. OBRE, DAVID MITCHELL'S
AUNT, THE ST. CHARLES HERALD
GUIDE, 2006

David's family disagreed with the coroner's assessment. They knew he was an excellent swimmer and wouldn't have drowned in a ditch, and they also claimed David rarely hitchhiked and did not have a "high-risk" lifestyle. David's mother said during high school, he was an honor roll student and a school newspaper reporter. Despite the coroner's report, David's family knew he had been murdered; the only question was, who would do such a thing?

~

Ronald Joseph Dominique was born into poverty on January 9th, 1964, in Thibodaux, Louisiana. His parents were laborers, and the family lived in a trailer park on the city's outskirts. The trailer was barely large enough to house the Dominique family, but Ronald's parents worked hard, and there was always food on the table.

A CHANGE IN PERSONALITY

As a teenager, Ronald mowed lawns for extra money, sang in the local glee club, and volunteered to help older people with groceries and other tasks.

He seemed outgoing, but Ronald went through bouts of mild depression and had low self-esteem as a teenager.

He was now dealing with another problem — his sexual identity. During his last year of high school, he frequented local gay bars. He was seen once by a class-mate who told others at school that Ronald was at the bar. He denied it for fear of being singled out and bullied.

Ronald graduated from Thibodaux High School in 1983 and enrolled at Nicholls State University to study computer science. It wasn't long before he dropped out.

Ronald's club lifestyle became essential to him. When he went to clubs, he often dressed in drag as his idol, Patti LaBelle. Despite being part of the community, people were uncomfortable with him, and he had trouble getting dates. He would occasionally get a paying gig to impersonate LaBelle on stage, and he'd use the money to pay men to have sex with him at the club.

Ronald also worked in low-level, low-skilled jobs where pay was minimal. He was often disciplined on the job and didn't stay employed for long. He was able to secure housing for himself, usually in a rented trailer, but more often than not, he lived off of the charity of relatives, most notably his mother and older sister.

His behavioral issues also continued outside of the workplace. On July 12th, 1985, he was arrested on charges of sexual harassment via telephone. And over a decade later, in 1996, he was arrested again when a nude young man jumped out of Ronald's trailer window and told neighbors Ronald had raped and then attempted to kill him. Ronald was arrested but later released when his alleged victim disappeared.

This period marked a pivotal change in Ronald's behavior. His actions escalated from engaging in paid sexual activities to committing acts of sexual violence. He became aware of what he could get away with. His victims were predominantly homeless African American men, many of whom struggled with drug and alcohol addiction and engaged in sex work to fund their habits. Ronald targeted these individuals specifically because he believed they wouldn't be noticed if they went missing. He embarked upon a nine-year killing spree, which started with the death of David Mitchell.

GARY PIERRE

Six months after the murder of David Mitchell, the remains of 20-year-old Gary Pierre were discovered in St. Charles Parish. Pierre was a known drug dealer and had been recently arrested on charges related to drug trafficking. The police assumed Pierre's death was related to his drug trafficking activities and closed the case quickly.

In July of 1998, the body of 38-year-old Larry Ranson was found. Ranson, who was a drug-addicted homeless man, was left bound on the side of the road. There was evidence of sexual assault that took place before Ranson was strangled to death.

When the body of the fourth victim, 27-year-old Oliver LeBanks, was discovered on the outskirts of Metairie on

October 4th of that same year, the police were able to collect semen that belonged to the perpetrator.

Over the subsequent eight years, a disturbing pattern emerged, as the bodies of men, whose ages varied from 16 to 46, were located in isolated settings such as sugar-cane fields, remote bayous, and ditches. In most cases, the men had been bound, strangled, and sexually assaulted. Ronald's youngest victim was 16-year-old Joseph Brown. He lured Joseph into his truck to sell him crack cocaine. After sharing the drugs with him, Ronald hit the teenager several times on the head with a blunt object and then strangled him with a plastic bag.

The police now had 23 murders possibly attributed to one person. They had a serial killer on their hands. They just couldn't identify him.

THE FINAL MURDER VICTIM

Twenty-seven-year-old Christopher Sutterfield met Ronald Dominique at a nightclub in the summer of 2006, and they began dating not long after that. In October, while on a date together in Iberville Parish, Ronald hit Christopher across the head with a blunt object and killed him. Christopher's family recalled seeing him with a man driving a black SUV, but they couldn't give the police a description of the man.

FORMATION OF THE BAYOU STRANGLER TASK FORCE

In March 2005, an interagency task force was established to examine the murders. This task force included representatives from nine South Louisiana parish sheriff's departments, the Louisiana State Police, and the FBI.

The 23 individuals who had been killed were predominantly homeless men. The cause of death in most of the cases involved asphyxiation or strangulation. A number of the deceased were also found without footwear. In eight of the murders, the investigators were able to collect samples of semen and blood from the crime scene, but these samples, all from the same person, had no match in the FBI's CODIS database.

CATCHING A KILLER

Ricky Wallace had a meeting with his parole officer, and in that meeting, he mentioned that earlier that year, he'd been lured to a trailer with the promise of drugs and an opportunity to have sex with a man's wife. Ricky knew Ronald Dominique's name and described him as a Caucasian man who was overweight and walked with a cane.

Ricky went with the man but turned him down when he realized the man had no wife and no drugs. He told his parole officer the man wanted to tie him up and then have sex with him. He said he left quickly after the man threatened him when he declined. The parole officer called the police to give them the information.

Ronald Dominique had recently relocated from his sister's house to the Bunkhouse shelter in Houma, Louisiana. While those who lived with Ronald at the shelter thought him strange, they never suspected he was a killer. Based on Ricky Wallace's statement, the police located Ronald and arrested him at the homeless shelter.

The police interviewed Ronald and followed this up by asking him to give a blood sample. The sample proved to be a match for several fluid samples taken from eight "Bayou Strangler" crime scenes. Ronald Domonique was formally arrested and charged with eight counts of first-degree murder.

Ronald entered the courthouse using his cane. It took him several minutes to get up to the arraignment desk. Outside the courtroom, his friends and family told the media that Ronald had suffered two heart attacks in the last two months.

The sheriff made his own statement, admitting that Ronald was under the care of a physician in the jail to monitor a minor heart condition. He asked the public to remember that he is accused of multiple murders in which he allegedly murdered young men and disposed of their bodies.

Ronald Dominique's bail was set at $8 million.

On December 1st, Ronald confessed to his crimes, telling police that he knew it was only a matter of time before he'd be captured. He gave details of each one of the murders he'd committed. As to why he had murdered, he said he needed to get rid of any witnesses and that each of the men voluntarily agreed to be bound. He said he let several men go when they refused such a request.

NO TRIAL

Following a plea deal to avoid the death penalty, Ronald Dominique entered a guilty plea to all eight counts of first-degree murder. On the 23rd of September, 2008, he received a sentence of eight life terms to be served consecutively.

Now 59, Ronald is presently incarcerated at the Louisiana State Penitentiary, commonly known as Angola.

Author's Note: Please see Appendix A for a complete list of the victims.

APPENDIX A

- David Mitchell 19 July 1997 St. Charles Parish
- Gary Pierre 20 December 1997 St. Charles Parish
- Larry Ranson 38 July 31, 1998 St. Charles Parish
- Oliver LeBanks 27 October 1998 Metairie, Jefferson Parish
- Joseph Brown 16 October 1998 Kenner, Jefferson Parish
- Bruce Williams 18 November 1998 Jefferson Parish
- Manuel Reed 21 May 1999 Kenner, Jefferson Parish
- Angel Mejia 34 June 1999 Kenner, Jefferson Parish
- Mitchell Johnson 34 August 1999 Metairie, Jefferson Parish
- Michael Vincent 23 January 2000 Lafourche Parish

- Kenneth Randolph, Jr. 20 October 2002 Lafourche Parish
- Anoka Jones 26 October 12, 2002 Houma, Terrebonne Parish
- Datrell Woods 19 May 24, 2003, Bayou Blue, Terrebonne Parish
- Larry Matthews 46 October 2004 Bayou Blue, Terrebonne Parish
- Michael Barnett 21 October 24, 2004, Bayou Blue, Terrebonne Parish
- Leon Lirette 22 February 2005 Bayou Blue, Terrebonne Parish
- August Watkins 31 April 2005 Lafourche Parish
- Kurt Cunningham 23 April 2005 Lafourche Parish
- Alonzo Hogan 28 July 2005 St. Charles Parish
- Wayne Smith 17 August 2005 Terrebonne Parish
- Chris Deville 40 September 2005 Assumption Parish
- Nicholas Pellegrin 21 November 2005 Lafourche Parish
- Christopher Sutterfield 27 October 2006 Iberville Parish

APPENDIX B

Women murdered by both Angelo Buono and Kenneth Bianchi

- Yolanda Washington, age 19 – October 17, 1977
- Judith Lynn Miller, age 15 – October 31, 1977
- Lissa Kastin, age 21 – November 5, 1977
- Jane King, age 28 – November 9, 1977
- Dolores Cepeda, age 12 – November 13, 1977
- Sonja Johnson, age 14 – November 13, 1977
- Kristina Weckler, age 20 – November 20, 1977
- Lauren Wagner, age 18 – November 28, 1977
- Kimberely Martin, age 17 – December 9, 1977
- Cindy Lee Hudspeth, age 20 – February 16, 1978

Women murdered by Kenneth Bianchi

- Karen Lauretta Mandic, age 20 — January 11, 1979

- Diane Amy Clark Wilder, age 27 —January 22, 1979

FROM FAMILY ANNIHILATORS: A MURDER STORY

Retired teacher and adoptee Kathy Gillcrist waited until she was close to sixty years old before seeking out her birth family. Growing up, she had no curiosity to know who her birth parents were or if she had other siblings. In retirement, she decided it would be an exciting project to tackle. She took a DNA test and waited for the results to come back. After looking at all her genetic "cousins," she contacted her third cousin, who was an amateur genealogist and asked for help.

After months of research, her cousin found her parents. While there was nothing particularly remarkable about her birthmother other than a liaison with her birthfather in 1956, her birthfather was a different story.

He was an accomplished, educated American diplomat who murdered his entire family in 1976 and escaped. The first picture she saw of him was an FBI "most wanted list" mugshot with the heading, "wanted for unlawful flight to avoid prosecution and murder with a blunt instrument."

The family likeness was undeniable. They had the same nose, mouth, and dimpled chin. They even shared a mole in the same spot on their face.

Kathy finally had the story of her parents. They were never married, and her mother was young and gave her up for adoption. Gillcrist's birth father may not have even known of her existence, as the family he created and murdered was after her birth in 1957. Her father's background intrigued her, and as her story surfaced in the local media, she was contacted by officials and other people connected with the case. She was shocked to discover that her father was only 21 when she was born. William Bishop could still be alive.

~

William Bradford Bishop Jr. was born on August 1st, 1936, in Pasadena, California, to Lobelia Amaryllis St. Germain and William Bradford Bishop Sr. He attended South Pasadena High School and went on to earn a bachelor's degree in history from Yale University as well as a master's degree in international studies from Middlebury College. Bishop also held a master's degree in African Studies from UCLA.

After graduating from Yale in 1959, Bishop married Annette Weis, his high school sweetheart, and then had three sons. He joined the United States Army and spent four years working in counterintelligence. Bishop was fluent in five languages: English, Italian, French, Spanish and Serbo-Croatian. After leaving the Army, he joined the U.S. State Department and served in the Foreign Service with numerous overseas postings. His family accompanied him on these postings. This included postings in the Italian cities of Verona, Milan, and Florence from 1968 to 1972, where he did postgraduate work at the University of Florence. He also served in Africa, with posts in Ethiopia and Botswana, from 1972 to 1974.

Bishop's final posting in 1974 was at the State Department in Washington, D.C. At the time, he was living in Bethesda, Maryland, with his wife, three sons, and his mother, Lobelia.

On March 1st, 1976, after learning he would not receive the promotion he had sought at the State Department, Bishop told his secretary that he was feeling unwell and left his office. This was the last confirmed sighting of Bishop by his colleague Roy Harrell, who noted that Bishop seemed agitated.

THE MURDER PLAN

Police believe Bishop drove to his bank, where he withdrew several hundred dollars before going to the Montgomery Mall. At the mall, he purchased a ball-peen hammer and gas can, which he used to fill up the can and the tank of his 1974 Chevrolet station wagon at a nearby gas station. Bishop then went to a hardware store to buy a shovel and pitchfork.

Between 7:30 and 8:00 pm, Bishop returned to his home in Bethesda. His wife, Annette, was likely killed first, followed by his mother, Lobelia, when she returned from walking the family dog. Finally, Bishop went upstairs and killed his three sleeping sons, Geoffrey, age 5, Brent, age 10, and Brad III, age 14. Bishop then loaded the bodies into the station wagon and drove 275 miles to a densely wooded area about 5 miles south of Columbia, North Carolina.

On March 2nd, Bishop dug a shallow hole and piled the bodies inside before dousing them with gasoline and setting them on fire. Discovered along with the burned bodies were a gas can, pitchfork, and shovel with a label from Poch's Hardware store.

Later that same day, Bishop was known to have purchased items at a sporting goods store in Jacksonville, North Carolina. According to witnesses, he had the family dog with him and may have been accompanied by an unidentified woman described only as "dark-skinned."

On March 10th, 1976, a neighbor who had not seen the Bishop family for some time contacted the police to do a welfare check. A detective was sent to the home, where he found blood on the front porch, floor, walls, and bedrooms.

Officers didn't realize that the bodies of the Bishop family had already been found in North Carolina on March 2nd. Forest Ranger Ronald Brickhouse discovered the bodies of the family after a fire spotter had reported smoke from a watchtower.

The bodies of Annette and her mother-in-law, Lobelia, were lying on top of the three boys. The women wore street clothes, and the boys were in pajamas. Each victim had a bloody towel wrapped around their head. The medical examiner said all had been beaten to death with a blunt instrument. Dental records later confirmed that the burned bodies discovered in North Carolina belonged to Bishop's wife, mother, and three sons.

ON THE RUN

On March 18th, Bishop's abandoned 1974 Chevrolet station wagon was found at an isolated campground in Elkmont, Tennessee. The car was located in Great Smoky Mountains National Park, just a few miles from the Appalachian Trail and about 400 miles from where the bodies had been buried in North Carolina. Authorities found dog biscuits, a bloody blanket, a shotgun, an ax, and a shaving kit containing Bishop's medication inside the car. The trunk's spare tire well was filled with blood. Based on witness statements, it was determined the car had been there for about two weeks.

"I have always held the theory that that car was placed in that location as a ruse. Bradford Bishop could be somewhere over at Chapel Hill with a beard walking around. Bradford Bishop, with his background, is capable of doing that…"

RUFUS EDMISTEN, NORTH CAROLINA ATTORNEY GENERAL, *THE CHARLOTTE OBSERVER*, APRIL 28TH, 1976

Police theorized that after abandoning the car, Bishop likely joined hikers on the Appalachian Trail in an attempt to disappear. However, attempts to track him using bloodhounds were unsuccessful. The next day, on March 19, 1976, a grand jury indicted Bishop on five counts of first-degree murder.

Bishop's motives for murdering his family have never been fully explained. Although Bishop had been passed over for a promotion, he had no history of problems at work and had had a successful career.

MOTIVE SPECULATION

It was reported that Bishop frequently faced criticism from his wife, Annette, age 37, and mother, Lobelia, age 68, over his lack of advancement at the State Department. Bishop was said to be unhappy with his desk job and wanted a foreign posting, but his wife was reluctant to move abroad again. Annette had started taking art classes at the University of Maryland despite Bishop wanting her to remain a stay-at-home mother.

Most sources agree the Bishops had some financial issues, but the extent is unclear. Some described them as mild and typical, while others reported the IRS was auditing the family due to money troubles.

Bishop had a history of depression and insomnia, for which he took medications. He was an avid outdoorsman who enjoyed camping and hiking. Bishop was also fond of dogs, scotch whiskey, and spicy foods. He had a six-inch surgical scar on his lower back, cleft chin, and facial mole. Bishop likely took his father's revolver and Yale class ring when he disappeared. Authorities believe he also took his diplomatic passport to avoid detection.

SIGHTINGS

In the over 40 years since the murders, there have been numerous reported sightings of Bishop across Europe, including Sweden, Italy, Belgium, England, Finland, the Netherlands, Germany, Greece, Spain, and Switzerland.

In July 1978, a Swedish woman who had worked with Bishop in Ethiopia claimed she saw him twice in one week at a public park in Stockholm. She did not contact the police at the time because she was unaware he was a wanted fugitive.

In January 1979, Bishop's former State Department colleague Roy Harrell reported seeing him in a restaurant restroom in Sorrento, Italy. When Harrell addressed the bearded man as Bishop, he denied his identity and quickly fled.

On September 19th, 1994, a former neighbor who knew the Bishops in Bethesda claimed to see Bishop up close on a train platform in Basel, Switzerland. She described him as well-groomed and said he later got into a car at the station.

Bishop's case has been featured extensively in media and television shows in recent decades. In 2010, authorities believed he likely lived in plain sight somewhere in Europe or California, possibly working as a teacher or involved in criminal activities.

Before the murders, Bishop had been corresponding with an Illinois federal prison inmate named Albert Kenneth Bankston for unknown reasons. Bankston died in 1983 without knowing of the murders or that Bishop was wanted.

In 2014, the FBI exhumed a John Doe killed in a 1981 Alabama car accident after speculation he could have been Bishop. However, DNA testing confirmed the man's identity was not a match. Authorities now believe Bishop resides in the U.S., and he avoids arrest to prevent his identification through fingerprints.

THE SEARCH CONTINUES

Forensic artist Karen Taylor created an age progression sculpture at the FBI's request to suggest what Bishop may look like around age 77. Using this sculpture, images were made showing Bishop with possible facial hair and glasses as disguises.

In early April 2014, WRC-TV in Washington D.C. launched a website displaying extensive information about the case, including samples of Bishop's handwriting, fingerprints, dental records, and previously unseen family videos.

The latest information in the case came from the positive DNA test from Kathy Gillcrist. It's possible that Bishop has had other children after murdering his family, and they may show up in databases as well.

While Bishop has managed to avoid capture for over

forty years, the confirmation he is likely still alive has energized law enforcement efforts. Authorities believe it is only a matter of time before he is finally arrested and made to answer for his crimes, even as an octogenarian.

Grab the *Curated True Crime Book Family Annihilators!* Family Annihilators

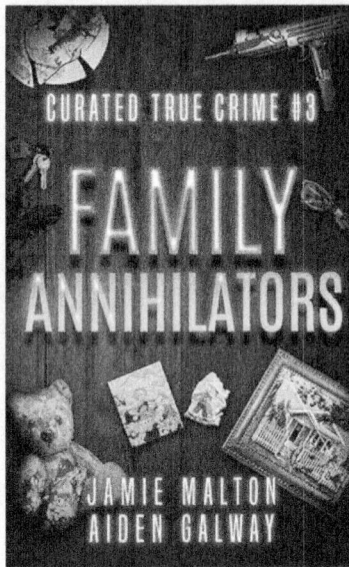

FREE TRUE CRIME AUDIO BOOK

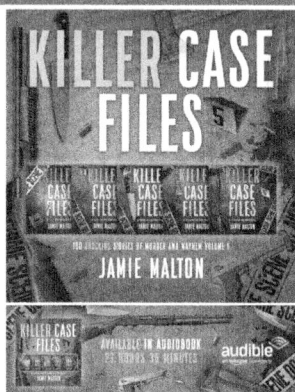

★★★★★
Great stories of amazing cases.
This is my first introduction to Jamie Malton. This girl can write. A lot of cases in this book I never heard of before but they were fascinating nonetheless. Looking forward to checking out the rest of her work.
James Herington

★★★★★
Best book on murder cases-recommend all Killer Case files books.
Loved how informative each story was. Excellent selection of stories. Enjoyed very much.
Carole DeCandido

★★★★★
Love this series.
Well, written and interesting collection.
Cheryl A.

★★★★★
Great read
Very good book detailing some of the more obscure stories of murder. It's amazing that these stories have not been told earlier.
bake904

★★★★★
An Excellent Read
I like everything about the book because it appears that the author took the time to select a variety of stories. Of course, this resulted in stories that are of interest to various true crime readers. I recommend this book to any fan of true crime stories.
Anne Thompson-Ellerbee

Sign up to Audible and use your free credit to access over 23 hours of Killer Case Files audio.

US: Get your Free Audiobook With This Link

UK: Get your Free Audiobook With This Link

FREE US CODE

FREE UK CODE

ABOUT THE AUTHOR

Jamie Malton is an award-winning author of true crime literature, known for her gritty, fact-driven narratives. Her books with their uncompromising portrayals of real crime have captivated readers of the genre.

Interested in real-life crime investigations, Malton writes about the intricacies of police work, DNA reconstruction, and genetic genealogy.

In her fifteen years as a digital nomad, she has traversed the globe, often venturing to the very locations where the crimes she details have unfolded. Her international journeys add layers of depth and authenticity to her writing.

Dedicated to the pursuit of justice, Malton goes beyond storytelling. She contributes a portion of her book sales to charities that aid in the DNA reconstruction for unsolved cases and provide support for the families of victims.

To delve into the world of true crime with Jamie Malton, visit her website at JamieMalton.com.

Printed in Great Britain
by Amazon

47148920R00079